CONTENTS

PREFACE

Welcome to a celebration of Pentecost! For far too long, Pentecost has been sorely deemphasized on Protestant church calendars after all the concentration spent on Christmas and Easter. Surely, those two celebrations are important observations of the incarnation and sacrifice that God endured to save His creation. But of no less importance is the event that marked the arrival of the Holy Spirit, when God breathed and mankind received His divine presence within their souls. If Christmas is "God with us" and Easter is "God died for us," then surely Pentecost is "God within us, always."

It is the Holy Spirit who instated the Church Age. It is the Holy Spirit who inspired the writing of God's Word, the Bible. And it is the Holy Spirit who continues to fall on believers, empowering them for ministry and confirming His work with signs, miracles, and wonders.

This was especially evident with the Pentecostal revival of the late nineteenth and early twentieth centuries, a movement of the Spirit that continues through this day. Early evangelical pioneers in church history like John Wesley, Charles Finney, R. A. Torrey, and D. L. Moody recognized the power of the Holy Spirit to convict sinners and bring them to Christ. But it was in the lives and ministries of men like Smith Wigglesworth, Andrew Murray, John G. Lake, and Derek Prince, as well as women like Aimee Semple MacPherson and Maria Woodworth-Etter, that a new manifestation of the Spirit began to emerge and spread. The Welsh and Azusa Street revivals, led by men like William Seymour, became catalysts that birthed a new expression of worship and a ministry emphasis on the use of spiritual gifts that included miraculous healings, speaking in tongues, prophetic declarations, and even the raising of the dead. The legacy of these early Pentecostal pioneers continues to this day.

Pentecost occurred fifty days after Jesus's resurrection. The fifty devotional readings in the *Tongues of Fire Devotional* is a rare collection of works by the leaders of the charismatic and Pentecostal movement, both historical and contemporary. We hope that celebrating the fifty days in anticipation of Pentecost will keep the old teachings alive, reveal how their legacies are being carried on today, and inspire the Holy Spirit-filled spiritual leaders of tomorrow. May it bring you a fresh encounter with the Holy Spirit, God within you.

—Whitaker House

INTRODUCTION:
THE SIGNIFICANCE OF PENTECOST

DEREK PRINCE

And suddenly there came a sound from heaven as of a rushing mighty wind, and it filled the house where they were sitting. Then there appeared to them cloven tongues like as of fire, and it sat upon each of them. And they were all filled with the Holy Ghost, and began to speak with other tongues, as the Spirit gave them utterance.
—Acts 2:2–4

During the day of Pentecost, there were one hundred and twenty-four believers waiting in an upper room. These men and women were praying to the Lord, until they came to the place where they were all of one accord.

After the Holy Spirit was poured out on these believers, people gathered around, drawn by "sounds from heaven." They heard these unlearned Galileans speaking perfectly and flawlessly in other languages. The crowd—filled with people from various regions and nations—knew that these men and women didn't know all those languages. Yet all those gathered were able to understand the wonderful works of God that were being declared in their own tongues.

Of course, the question arose, "Whatever could this mean?" Some people mocked them and said they were drunk, but Peter stood up and answered them:

> *Men of Judea and all you that dwell at Jerusalem, let this be known to you, and harken to my words: for these are not drunken, as you suppose, seeing it is but the third hour of the day. But this is that which was spoken by the prophet Joel; And it shall come to pass in the last days, says God, I will pour out of My Spirit upon all flesh: and your sons and your daughters shall prophesy, and your young men shall see visions, and your old men shall dream dreams: and on My servants and on My handmaidens I will pour out in those days My Spirit; and they shall prophesy: and I will show wonders in heaven above, and signs in the earth beneath; blood, and fire, and vapor of smoke: the sun shall be turned into darkness, and the moon into blood, before that great and notable day of the Lord come: and it shall come to pass, that whosoever shall call on the name of the Lord shall be saved.* (Acts 2:14–21)

Peter, by inspiration of the Holy Spirit, immediately referred to the prophecy found in the second chapter of the book of Joel. This divine inspiration is one of the remarkable incidents that happened on the day of Pentecost. Until that time, the apostles had a very limited, and sometimes unclear, understanding of the Scriptures. Many times, Jesus had to explain to them what they could not comprehend from His teachings. But the moment the Holy Spirit came upon them, the apostles' grasp of the Scriptures dramatically changed. This baptism by the Spirit enabled Peter to stand up and give the sermon that is recorded in the book of Acts.

I want to relate segments of Peter's sermon to their prophetic relevance for our present day. Peter said: *"And it shall come to pass in the last days, says God, I will pour out of My Spirit upon all flesh: and your sons and your daughters shall prophesy, and your young men shall see visions…: I will pour out in those days of My Spirit; and they shall prophesy."*

Please note a factor revealed in these verses that is particularly relevant to our current society. That factor is the tremendous emphasis on young people. Out of the four groups specified in Acts 2:17, three are specifically young people—*"your sons," "your daughters,"* and *"your young men."* This is not an accident. I believe we are currently looking at a situation that may never have happened before in history: young people make up the majority of our population.

We need to recognize that there will be special satanic pressures and evil forces directed against these young people. But God has given provision for His young people through the fullness of the Holy Spirit. Every Christian young person needs the indwelling of the Holy Spirit to survive these latter days.

For those who have been taught that the outpouring of the Holy Spirit was only for a certain limited time during the early church age, I want to remind you that Peter said, *"In the last days…."* Let me ask you this question: Have we gone beyond the "last days"? If it was the last days when Peter spoke, how much further along are we in the last days today?

Thus, if there were supernatural manifestations of the Holy Spirit then, *how much more* are we to expect them now? Not how much less, but how much *more*. The Scripture specifically says, *"In the last days…I will pour out of My Spirit…. Your sons and your daughters shall prophesy, and your young men shall see visions."* There is no interpretation of this verse that suggests these signs were only for the early church and are therefore out-of-date for today. This mind-set goes directly contrary to the plain statement of Scripture.

I believe by looking at the original prophesy of Joel, we can better understand Peter's statements.

> *Be glad then, you children of Zion, and rejoice in the* Lord *your God; for He has given you the former rain moderately, and He will cause to come down for you the rain, the former rain, and the latter rain in the first month.* (Joel 2:23)

Please notice that this prophecy leads to the outpouring of the Holy Spirit. It is perfectly clear we have scriptural authority for saying that the rain mentioned here is a metaphor for the Holy Spirit. According to Joel, the rains are divided up into two out-pourings—the former rain and the latter (or the last) rain. This description is the key to understanding the application of this prophecy to the days in which we live.

The promise of the former rain to God's people was fulfilled on the day of Pentecost. This first outpouring of the Holy Spirit, according to Scripture, lasted between one to two centuries. It is recorded in the book of Acts, and elsewhere, with demonstrations of supernatural signs, manifestations, and power.

Then the former rain dried up, and we entered into the winter season—when rain falls, but only from time to time in scattered places. This is true of church history, in which we discover there was no stoppage of the outpouring of the Holy Spirit. From time to time, in different places and in different areas, the Holy Spirit would manifest in certain groups of people with evidence of signs and miracles following.

We continue through the winter season until we come to the Passover month, or what corresponds to the first month. This is the new beginning and the latter (or the last) rain. What is God going to do with the latter rain? Joel 2:23 speaks about the former rain, and then verse 25 says, "*I will restore to you the years that the locust has eaten.*" This outpouring of the latter rain will restore to God's people what has been lost to them over the past centuries.

What is our next step after this restoration? We find the answer to this question in Jeremiah 5:24:

> Let us now fear the LORD our God, that gives rain, both the former and the latter, in His season: He reserves to us the appointed weeks of the harvest.

The Lord has given the latter rain for the harvest, for the ingathering of souls, which is the consummation of God's purposes in the earth. When the harvest comes, it is for a short period of time—an urgent period of time. It is the busiest time of the year for those involved. The Lord says that He has reserved to us the appointed weeks, a short period of time, for this harvest of souls. We cannot delay, we cannot postpone, and we cannot say it doesn't suit us to do this now. Why? After this harvest, the Lord will return. James 5:7–8 says:

> Be patient therefore, brethren, to the coming of the Lord. Behold, the husbandman waits for the precious fruit of the earth, and has long patience for it, until he receive the early and latter rain. Be you also patient; establish your hearts: for the coming of the Lord draws near.

After the latter rain comes the harvest. According to James, this harvest is connected to the coming of the Lord. This outpouring of the Holy Spirit in the latter rain is the greatest indication that the Lord Jesus is ready to come back.

In closing, let me ask you a few personal questions. Where do you stand on this matter? Will you decide to receive the only power that will enable a Christian to endure in these last days? Will you be part of the last great harvest? May it be said of those who are, "These are the ones who have turned the world upside down." (See Acts 17:6.)

DAY 1

THE FULLNESS OF THE SPIRIT

SMITH WIGGLESWORTH

In those days will I pour out My Spirit.
—Joel 2:29

God wants you to be so balanced in spiritual anointing that you will always be able to do what pleases Him, and not what will please other people or yourself. The ideal must be that it will all be to edification, and everything must go to this end to please the Lord.

"Follow after charity, and desire spiritual gifts, but rather that you may prophesy" (1 Corinthians 14:1). When someone came to Moses and said that there were two others in the camp prophesying, Moses said, *"Would God that all the LORD's people were prophets, and that the LORD would put His spirit upon them!"* (Numbers 11:29). That is a clear revelation along these lines that God wants us to be in such a spiritual, holy place that He could take our words and so fill them with divine power that we would speak only as the Spirit leads in prophetic utterances.

Beloved, there is spiritual language, and there is also human language, which always stays on the human plane. The divine comes into the same language so that it is changed by spiritual power and brings life to those who hear you speak. But this divine touch of prophecy will never come in any way except through the infilling of the Spirit.

If you wish to be anything for God, do not miss His plan. God has no room for you on ordinary lines. You must realize that within you, there is the power of the Holy Spirit, who is forming within you everything you require.

I believe we have too much preaching and too little testifying. You will never have a living Pentecostal church with a preacher who, every night, is preaching, preaching, preaching. The people get tired of this constant preaching, but they never get tired when the whole place is on fire, when twenty or more jump up at once and will not sit down until they testify. So remember, you must awaken out of your lethargy.

> *And it shall come to pass afterward, that I will pour out My Spirit upon all flesh; and your sons and your daughters shall prophesy, your old men shall dream dreams, your young men shall see visions: and also upon the menservants and upon the handmaidens in those days will I pour out My Spirit.*
>
> (Joel 2:28–29)

This was spoken by the prophet Joel, and we know that this is what occurred on the Day of Pentecost. This was the first outpouring of the Spirit, but what would it be like now if we would only wake up to the words of our Master, *"Greater works than these shall* [you] *do; because I go to My Father"* (John 14:12)?

Hear what the Scripture says to us: *"However when He, the Spirit of truth, is come, He will guide you into all truth: for He shall not speak of Himself; but whatsoever He shall hear, that shall He speak"* (John 16:13). The Holy Spirit is inspiration; the Holy Spirit is revelation; the Holy Spirit is manifestation; the Holy Spirit is operation. When a man comes into the fullness of the Holy Spirit, he is in perfect order, built up on scriptural foundations.

I have failed to see any man understand the twelfth, thirteenth, and fourteenth chapters of 1 Corinthians unless he had been baptized with the Holy Spirit. He may talk about the Holy Spirit and the gifts, but his understanding is only a superficial one. However, when he gets baptized with the Holy Spirit, he speaks about a deep, inward conviction by the power of the Spirit working in him, a revelation of that Scripture. On the other hand, there is so much that a man receives when he is born again. He receives the first love and has a revelation of Jesus. *"But if we walk in the light, as He is in the light, we have fellowship one with another, and the blood of Jesus Christ His Son cleanses us from all sin"* (1 John 1:7).

But God wants a man to be on fire so that he will always speak as an oracle of God. He wants to so build that man on the foundations of God that everyone who sees and hears him will say he is a new man after the order of the Spirit. *"Old things are passed away; behold, all things are become new"* (2 Corinthians 5:17). New things have come, and he is now in the divine order. When a man is filled with the Holy Spirit, he has a vital power that makes people know he has seen God. He ought to be in such a place spiritually that when he goes into a neighbor's house, or out among people, they will feel that God has come into their midst.

What we need is more of the Holy Spirit. Oh, beloved, it is not merely a measure of the Spirit, it is a pressed-down measure. It is not merely a pressed-down measure, it is *"shaken together, and running over"* (Luke 6:38). Anybody can hold a full cup, but you cannot hold an overflowing cup, and the baptism of the Holy Spirit is an overflowing cup. Praise the Lord!

DAY 2

HOLY SPIRIT, YOU ARE WELCOME HERE!

JAMES W. GOLL

*The Spirit of the L*ORD *will rest on Him, the spirit of wisdom and understanding, the spirit of counsel and strength, the spirit of knowledge and the fear of the L*ORD.
—Isaiah 11:2 NASB

Oh, how I love the Holy Spirit! He makes Jesus real! He makes the Father enjoyable! I roll out the red carpet to this precious Dove of God every day. I say, "Holy Spirit, You are welcome here!"

The Holy Spirit is the One who connects us to heaven. Without Him, not even Jesus could have known what the Father wanted Him to say or to do. (See, for example, John 5:19.) If you want to know God, you absolutely *must* get to know the Holy Spirit, who works tirelessly to connect heaven and earth.

This Holy Spirit is described in the Scriptures as the "Spirit of Knowledge," which means that He is the Spirit of knowing and of being known. In other words, the Spirit has been given to us to make God known and to make Him knowable. Father God is approachable, but without the Holy Spirit's help, we tend to be afraid of Him. We are afraid because of our sin. But we can approach God without trepidation when we are in Christ (see Hebrews 4:15–16), having the Holy Spirit as our Helper, because the Spirit is our Comforter, or *Paraclete* (from the Greek *paráklētos*, "close-beside," and "make a call," like a legal advocate who makes the right judgment call, being close to the situation). The Spirit is our Advocate and Encourager.

Isaiah noted that [Jesus] would be filled with the Spirit of God, and the prophet expanded on what kind of Spirit this would be:

The Spirit of the LORD *will rest on Him, the spirit of wisdom and understanding, the spirit of counsel and strength, the spirit of knowledge and the fear of the* LORD.

(Isaiah 11:2 NASB)

The Holy Spirit had an intimate relationship with the Messiah, *Yeshua*, during His ministry on earth. Jesus humbled Himself, becoming entirely dependent upon the Holy Spirit in order to do and say only those things that would please the Father. Just think about His life. Jesus was conceived and born of the Holy Spirit. The Spirit led Him. The Spirit anointed Him for His ministry at His baptism. Everything Jesus did, from resisting temptation in the wilderness to raising the dead, He did by the guidance and power of the Spirit. He offered Himself as a sacrifice by the Spirit. He was raised from the dead by the power of the Spirit. And, so that His followers could truly follow in His footsteps, Jesus was faithful to send His Spirit to them on the day of Pentecost (and to everyone since that time who has believed in Him, stepping into faith and becoming a child of God).

Because Jesus has bestowed the Holy Spirit on those who believe, we can have the Spirit of Knowledge, the Comforter, the

Advocate as close to us as our next breath, and He will help us to know God daily. (See, for example, John 15:26.)

Nobody will ever force you into a relationship with God, not even God Himself, although the Holy Spirit is the One who brings God's righteousness to bear on people. His methods, while persuasive and effective, are never coercive. He is the Helper and Caretaker, not a tyrant or a patrol cop. Most of His endeavors can be characterized by action verbs. He *indwells*, He *fills*, He *frees*, He *equips*, He *transforms*, He *convicts*, He *assures*, He *inspires*, He *guides* and *directs*, He *regenerates*—and He *resurrects*. That's a lot!

You don't have to wait until something happens spiritually before responding to the Holy Spirit. It is OK to seek Him out in order to instigate action. He likes it when you pursue Him. (Think of the way Jesus responded to the centurion in Luke 7:1–10.) God loves passionate pursuers!

Give the Holy Spirit the freedom and liberty to give you freedom and liberty. *"Now the Lord is the Spirit, and where the Spirit of the Lord is, there is liberty (emancipation from bondage, freedom)"* (2 Corinthians 3:17 AMP).

The often-quiet Holy Spirit is not a retiring Spirit—He is an activist. He is the dynamic power that Jesus promised to the church before Pentecost. He executes the purposes and plans of the Godhead. As the One who carries out God's purposes—His creativity, inspiration, conviction, regeneration, generosity, enlightenment, sanctification, and much more—He is always working. (See John 5:17.) Simply by paying attention to what He is doing and by cooperating with Him, we come to understand God better.

DAY 3

THE PERSON OF THE HOLY SPIRIT

R. A. TORREY

*But God has revealed them to us by His Spirit: for the Spirit
searches all things, yea, the deep things of God.
For what man knows the things of a man,
save the spirit of man which is in him? even so the things of
God knows no man, but the Spirit of God.*
—1 Corinthians 2:10–11

What are the distinctive characteristics, or marks, of personality?
Knowledge, feeling or emotion, and will. Any entity that thinks and
feels and wills is a person. When we say that the Holy Spirit is a
person, there are those who understand us to mean that the Holy
Spirit has hands and feet and eyes and ears and mouth and so on,
but these are not the characteristics of personality but of bodily sub-
stance. All of these characteristics or marks of personality are repeat-
edly ascribed to the Holy Spirit in the Old and New Testaments.

In our reading in 1 Corinthians, knowledge is ascribed to
the Holy Spirit. We are clearly taught that the Holy Spirit is not

merely an influence that illuminates our minds to comprehend the truth but also a being who Himself knows the truth.

We also read, *"But all these works that one and the selfsame Spirit, dividing to every man severally as He will"* (1 Corinthians 12:11). Here, will is ascribed to the Spirit, and we are taught that the Holy Spirit is not a power that we get hold of and use according to our desires but a Person of sovereign majesty who uses us according to His will. This distinction is of fundamental importance in our getting into right relations with the Holy Spirit. It is at this very point that many honest seekers after power and efficiency in service go astray. They are reaching out after and struggling to get possession of some mysterious and mighty power that they can make use of in their work according to their own desires. They will never get possession of the power they seek until they come to recognize that there is not some divine power for them to get hold of and use in their blindness and ignorance but that there is a person, infinitely wise as well as infinitely mighty, who is willing to take possession of them and use them according to His own perfect will.

When we stop to think of it, we must rejoice that there is no divine power we beings, so ignorant and so liable to err as we are, can get hold of and use. How appalling might be the results if there were. But what a holy joy must come into our hearts when we grasp the thought that there is a divine Person, One who never errs, who is willing to take possession of us and impart to us such gifts as He sees best and to use us according to His wise and loving will.

We read in Romans 8:27, *"He that searches the hearts knows what is the mind of the Spirit, because He makes intercession for the saints according to the will of God."* In this passage, mind is ascribed to the Holy Spirit. The Greek word translated *"mind"* is a comprehensive word, including the ideas of thought, feeling, and purpose. It is the same word that is used in Romans 8:7, where we read that *"the carnal mind is enmity against God: for it is not subject to the law of God, neither indeed can be."* So, in this verse, all the distinctive marks of personality are included in the word *mind* and are ascribed to the Holy Spirit.

We find the personality of the Holy Spirit brought out in a most touching and suggestive way in Romans 15:30: *"Now I beseech you, brethren, for the Lord Jesus Christ's sake, and for the love of the Spirit, that you strive together with me in your prayers to God for me."* Here we have *"love"* ascribed to the Holy Spirit. The reader would do well to stop and ponder those five words—*"the love of the Spirit."* We dwell often upon the love of God the Father. It is the subject of our daily and constant thought. We dwell often upon the love of Jesus Christ the Son. Who would think of calling himself a Christian who passed a day without meditating on the love of his Savior, but how often have we meditated upon *"the love of the Spirit"*?

There is perhaps no passage in the entire Bible in which the personality of the Holy Spirit comes out more tenderly and touchingly than in the following: *"And grieve not the Holy Spirit of God, whereby you are sealed unto the day of redemption"* (Ephesians 4:30). Here, grief is ascribed to the Holy Spirit. The Holy Spirit is not a blind, impersonal influence or power that comes into our lives to illuminate, sanctify, and empower us. No, He is immeasurably more than that. He is a holy Person who comes to dwell in our hearts, One who sees clearly every act we perform, every word we speak, every thought we entertain, even the most fleeting fancy that is allowed to pass through our minds. If there is anything in act or word or deed that is impure, unholy, unkind, selfish, mean, petty, or untrue, this infinitely Holy One is deeply grieved by it. I know of no thought that will help one more than this to lead a holy life and to walk softly in the presence of the Holy One.

DAY 4

THE HOLY SPIRIT BAPTISM IS FOR POWER

BILL JOHNSON

Nevertheless I tell you the truth; It is expedient for you that I go away: for if I go not away, the Comforter will not come to you; but if I depart, I will send Him to you.
—John 16:7

Jesus gave power and authority to His disciples, enabling them to function as He did. They operated as His deputies during His three and a half years of earthly ministry, empowered to influence the world with the gifts given to Jesus by His heavenly Father. The word *deputy* means "spokesperson, understudy, and delegate." They filled that role well. The encounters and commissions that Jesus had received were not yet their experience, yet they were able to function under His commission through their submission to His mission.

As a result, Jesus sent them to their hometowns to minister as He would, but without Him present. There seems to be strong evidence that the twelve soon-to-be-apostles were quite surprised by their own success as they brought back story after story of sick-nesses healed and demons expelled. At this moment, the disciples became the servants who could demonstrate God's unfolding redemptive plan. It revealed that God's salvation would heal the whole man: spirit, soul, and body.

Later, the disciples were shocked when Jesus said He was leav-ing them to return to the Father. They were even more shocked when Jesus said it would be better for them if He actually did go, because the Holy Spirit would be given to each of them. It's hard to imagine anything better than having Jesus with you in the flesh. But this promise of the Holy Spirit is so huge that if it is not our reality, it simply means that we are not living in the fullness of what God has made available through His abiding presence.

The apostles operated under the authority and power that Jesus had been given. But now that He was gone to be with the Father, they would have to get authority and power for themselves. And this was to be done the same way Jesus got it. *Authority comes in the commission,* and *power comes in the encounter.*

After His resurrection, Jesus appeared to the remaining eleven disciples. When He did, He announced that all authority had been given to Him. He then commissioned them to carry the good news of the kingdom of God. Authority was given to the apostles in this commission. But it must be noted that these same eleven disciples, who had already received the Holy Spirit when Jesus breathed on them (see John 20:19–22), were told to not leave Jerusalem until they had been *"endued [*"clothed" NIV] *with power from on high"* (Luke 24:49). They lacked the second part of what Jesus carried: power. Just as Jesus received power at His water baptism when the Holy Spirit came upon Him in the form of a dove and remained, so His followers would need to be clothed with power through their own Holy Spirit baptism. This took place in Acts 2:4.

I am Pentecostal. Those are my roots. It's a heritage for which I am very thankful. But many in my history fall short of God's intention. Let me explain: As much as I am thankful for the ability to pray in tongues—for personal edification, praise, and prayer—this Holy Spirit baptism is for power. Pure and simple. There are many who can demonstrate certain gifts of the Spirit, but they do not walk in power. Demons and disease can only be dealt with by people who have experienced the same baptism that Jesus received, the one He promised to those who follow Him. Without it, we create reasons for these infirmities of the body and soul to remain. Tragically, many stop short of the divine encounter they need because they are satisfied with good theology. And, as good as that may seem, truth must lead us to the person—*Jesus*. Only Jesus can give us the Holy Spirit baptism. The reality of that baptism can only be measured in the power of God through our lives.

There were one hundred twenty people in the upper room. Suddenly, they were all filled with the Holy Spirit. None were excluded. And yet, in Acts 4:31, which was probably a few years later, some of these same disciples are baptized in power again. The point is, there's always more. The power of God is seen in miracles. But it is also seen in the endurance needed until the miracle comes. That part of the subject must not be overlooked.

This power gives us a taste of the world to come, which ruins us for anything less. Jesus lived the normal Christian life in a way that must be followed. We must be the generation that picks up our cross and quits making excuses for powerless Christianity. The Spirit of the resurrected Christ lives in us. Powerlessness is now inexcusable.

We must be thankful for the measures of breakthrough we've seen, while at the same time hungry for the more of God. Until people are healed by touching our clothing, or delivered by falling under our shadow, there is more to be had. Let's become the generation that hungers for all that is now possible.

DAY 5

A DIVINE OUTPOURING

ANDREW MURRAY

I indeed have baptized you with water: but He shall baptize you with the Holy Ghost.
—Mark 1:8

The work of Christ points to the outpouring of the Holy Spirit. The preliminary stages were the mystery of the incarnation in Bethlehem, the great redemption accomplished on Calvary, the revelation of Christ as the Son of God by the resurrection, and His entrance into glory in the ascension. Their goal and their crown was the coming down of the Holy Spirit.

The church has hardly acknowledged this and has not seen that the glory of Pentecost is the highest glory of the Father and the Son. That is why the Holy Spirit has not yet been able to reveal and glorify the Son in the church as He would like. Let us see if we can realize what Pentecost means.

God made man in His own image and in His likeness with the distinct purpose that he should become like Himself. Man was to be a temple for God to dwell in. He was to become the home in which God could rest. The close, intimate union with man was what the Holy One longed for and looked forward to.

What was symbolized in the temple in Israel became a divine reality in Jesus of Nazareth. There was a human nature in Jesus, possessed by the divine Spirit. God would have it so with all men who accept Jesus and His Spirit as their life.

Christ's death was to remove the curse and power of sin and make it possible for man to receive His Spirit. His resurrection was the entrance of a perfected human nature into the life of deity, the divine Spirit-life. At His ascension, He was admitted as man into the very glory of God—the participation by human nature of perfect fellowship with God in glory in the unity of the Spirit.

And yet, with all this, the work was not yet complete. God's main purpose was still not fulfilled. How could the Father dwell in men even as He had dwelt in Christ? This was the great question to which Pentecost gives the answer.

The Holy Spirit is now sent forth in a new character and a new power, such as He never had come before. In creation and nature, He came forth from God as the Spirit of life. In the creation of man, He especially acted as the power in which man's Godlikeness was based. After man's fall, the Spirit still testified for God. In Israel, He appeared as the Spirit of the theocracy, distinctly inspiring and equipping certain men for their work. In Jesus Christ, He came as the Spirit of the Father given to Jesus without measure. All these are manifestations in different degrees of one and the same Spirit.

But now comes the long-promised and entirely new manifestation of the divine Spirit. The Spirit that has dwelt in the obedient life of Jesus Christ has taken up His human spirit into perfect fellowship and unity with Himself. He is now the Spirit of the exalted God-man. The man Christ Jesus enters the glory of God and the full fellowship of that Spirit-life in which God dwells. He receives from the Father the right to send forth His Spirit into His disciples—to Himself descend in the Spirit and dwell in them.

The Spirit comes in a new power that had not been possible before because Jesus had not been crucified or glorified. This new power is the very Spirit of the glorified Jesus. The work of the Son and the longing of the Father received its fulfillment. Man's heart has become the home of his God.

The mystery of the incarnation at Bethlehem is indeed glorious. A pure, holy body was formed for the Son of God. In that body, the Holy Spirit dwelt. This is indeed a miracle of divine power. This is a mystery of grace that passes all understanding. This is the blessing Pentecost brings and receives.

The entrance of the Son of God into our flesh in Bethlehem, His entrance into the curse and death of sin, His entrance into the very glory of the Father—these were but the preparatory steps. All these were accomplished so that the word could be fulfilled: "*Behold, the tabernacle of God is with men, and He will dwell with them*" (Revelation 21:3).

The narrative of the outpouring of the Spirit can be understood only in the light of all that preceded Pentecost. God did not think any sacrifice was too great to make it possible for Him to dwell with sinful men. This is the earthly reflection of Christ's exaltation in heaven, the participation He gives to His friends of the glory He now has with the Father.

DAY 6

KEYS TO RECEIVING THE BAPTISM OF THE HOLY SPIRIT

JOSHUA MILLS

Every one that asks receives; and he that seeks finds; and to him that knocks it shall be opened. If a son shall ask bread of any of you that is a father, will he give him a stone? or if he ask a fish, will he for a fish give him a serpent? Or if he shall ask an egg, will he offer him a scorpion? If you then, being evil, know how to give good gifts to your children: how much more shall your heavenly Father give the Holy Spirit to them that ask Him?
—Luke 11:10–13

The Scriptures tell us that after the move of the Holy Spirit filled those who were gathered in the upper room, they received a supernatural enablement with signs, wonders, and miracles following, and many people were added to the church on a daily basis.

This is what the baptism in the Holy Spirit will do. It brings the enablement to work the works of God. We are hooked up to the power source of heaven through the baptism in the Holy Spirit! *"But you shall receive power, after that the Holy Ghost is come upon you: and you shall be witnesses to Me"* (Acts 1:8). The baptism in the Holy Spirit releases us into the flow of heaven. It opens up the glory realm for us. The Bible says that when this fresh touch of the Holy Spirit comes upon us, we will receive a dynamite-type power from on high. This explosive power contains enough force to blow out any obstacle of the enemy! Without the baptism, we will never be able to live up to our full potential in Christ. We must receive the baptism in the Holy Spirit in order to function as the witnesses that God has created us to be.

I want to give you some keys for receiving the baptism in the Holy Spirit. If you desire to receive it, all you need to do is ask the Holy Spirit to come and fill you and live inside you with His power. It's that easy. Let me show it to you within the Word of God and give you some practical advice from experience.

Read Jesus's words from Luke 11:9–13:

Ask, and it shall be given you; seek, and you shall find; knock, and it shall be opened to you. For every one that asks receives; and he that seeks finds; and to him that knocks it shall be opened. If a son shall ask bread of any of you that is a father, will he give him a stone? or if he ask a fish, will he for a fish give him a serpent? Or if he shall ask an egg, will he offer him a scorpion? If you then, being evil, know how to give good gifts to your children: how much more shall your heavenly Father give the Holy Spirit to them that ask Him?

The Bible says that our heavenly Father will give the Holy Spirit to those who ask for Him! As I've ministered around the world, I've had people come to me who feel they didn't have a real baptism experience because when they prayed for the baptism in the Holy Spirit, they didn't immediately begin to speak in an unknown tongue. The problem has often been that they expected the results to be almost mechanical and automatic in nature.

Have you ever seen a baby who is learning how to speak? That tiny little baby begins to babble all sorts of sounds and noises trying to learn the proper words of speech. I remember when we were attempting to teach our son, Lincoln, how to speak when he was a baby. I was trying to get him to learn how to say "Daddy." I wanted so badly for him to speak! As he was learning this new word, he made many goo-goo and ga-ga sounds, until finally he spit out the word "Dadu!" I remember the feeling I had when he first said this. It wasn't completely correct pronunciation, but I loved it nonetheless because he was doing everything he could to say something he had never said before. He wanted to say my name! I loved it so much that I let him continue to use that name. From that time until now, Lincoln still calls me "Dadu"—and I love it!

So you're asking, what does this have to do with receiving the baptism in the Holy Spirit? When God desires to give us a new language, we must open up our mouths in order for Him to fill it. When we pray for the baptism in the Holy Spirit and we *believe* that we have received what we have prayed for, we can open up our mouth and trust that God will begin to fill it with his supernatural tongue. Open up your mouth and God will fill it. At first, it might sound like a bunch of goo-goos and ga-gas, but as you yield to the Spirit of God, suddenly you will break through into a free-flowing current of heavenly language that has no end! *"I am the LORD your God…open your mouth wide, and I will fill it"* (Psalm 81:10).

Now, your step of faith is to open up your mouth and begin speaking syllables that you don't necessarily understand. This is just like a baby beginning to speak. This is putting your faith into action. You can trust that the Holy Spirit within you will control what you say and make it into a beautiful heavenly prayer language. Sometimes you may only get one or two words at a time. Let the Holy Spirit develop this language for you—it will come word by word, from faith to faith! The baptism in the Holy Spirit will give you results! Get filled and get ready to be used of God in ways you've never dreamed of before! You will overcome any doubting or critical spirits that may try to hinder you from this experience by staying focused on the Word of God.

DAY 7

TEN REASONS TO SPEAK IN TONGUES

MYLES MUNROE

When [the disciples] heard this, they were baptized in the name of the Lord Jesus. And when Paul had laid his hands upon them, the Holy Ghost came on them; and they spoke with tongues, and prophesied.
—Acts 19:5–6

There is more to being filled with the Spirit than speaking in tongues, but tongues are an integral and important part of the manifestation of the Governor's [Holy Spirit's] presence in our lives. Speaking in tongues is a flowing stream that should never dry up. It will enrich and build up our spiritual lives. In my experience, speaking in tongues is a critical key in releasing and using other gifts of the Spirit. This, of course, applies to the gift of interpretation of tongues, but also to the other gifts, particularly prophecy, wisdom, and knowledge because they involve language.

Let's briefly look at ten reasons why every kingdom citizen should speak in tongues.

1. A SIGN OF CONNECTION TO THE KINGDOM

Tongues are often the initial supernatural evidence of the indwelling and filling of the Spirit. We see this first in the experience of the followers of Jesus at Pentecost. We also see it in the kingdom service of Paul of Tarsus. The physician Luke wrote, in the book of Acts, "*While Apollos was at Corinth, Paul took the road through the interior and arrived at Ephesus. There he found some disciples*" (Acts 19:1 NIV).

Notice that they were called "*disciples.*" They were actually followers of John the Baptist, and Paul said to them, in effect, "You are on the right track, but you need to hear about Jesus, the one whom John was referring to, and you need the promise that He provided for you. You need the baptism in the Holy Spirit."

When these disciples heard the gospel of the kingdom, which John had pointed them toward, and which Paul fully explained to them, they were baptized in water in the name of the Lord Jesus. When Paul placed his hands on them and prayed for them, the Holy Spirit came upon them, and they immediately spoke in tongues and prophesied. (See our feature verse for the day.)

An evidence that we are connected to the home country is that we receive heaven-given languages.

2. FOR EDIFICATION

Speaking in tongues builds up, or recharges, our spirits. We are personally strengthened as we interact with the King [God] through the Governor [the Holy Spirit]. As Paul wrote, "*He who speaks in a tongue edifies himself*" (1 Corinthians 14:4 NKJV). Tongues are given to us so that our communication with God can be as it was for Adam—with no interference.

3. TO REMIND US OF THE GOVERNOR'S INDWELLING PRESENCE

Tongues make us aware of the indwelling presence of the Holy Spirit, and when we are conscious of His presence, we are encouraged and comforted. Jesus said,

> And I will ask the Father, and he will give you another Counselor to be with you forever—the Spirit of truth. The world cannot accept him, because it neither sees him nor knows him. But you know him, for he lives with you and will be in you.   (John 14:16–17 NIV)

4. TO KEEP OUR PRAYERS IN LINE WITH THE KING'S WILL

Praying in tongues will keep our prayers in line with God's will and prevent us from praying in selfishness.

> The Spirit intercedes for the saints in accordance with God's will.   (Romans 8:27 NIV)

5. TO STIMULATE FAITH

Praying in tongues stimulates faith. When we know the Spirit is fully communicating our needs, we are enabled to trust God more completely. Having faith also leads to praying in tongues as we go to the throne of the King-Father in purpose and confidence. The author of the New Testament book of Jude wrote this about faith and speaking in tongues: "But you, dear friends, build yourselves up in your most holy faith and pray in the Holy Spirit" (Jude 20 NIV).

6. TO KEEP US FREE FROM WORLDLY CONTAMINATION

Tongues keep us in constant connection with the culture of the kingdom, even as we live in the midst of the culture of the world. Our connection with the King through the Governor helps to keep our minds and actions pure. We can also encourage not only ourselves but also others in the ways of the kingdom through heavenly communication. Paul wrote, *"Speaking to yourselves in psalms and hymns and spiritual songs, singing and making melody in your heart to the Lord"* (Ephesians 5:19).

7. TO ENABLE US TO PRAY FOR THE UNKNOWN

The Spirit knows things we know nothing about; therefore, through heaven-given language, we can intercede with peace and confidence. Again, *"we know not what we should pray for as we ought: but the Spirit Itself makes intercession for us with groanings which cannot be uttered"* (Romans 8:26).

8. TO GIVE SPIRITUAL REFRESHING

Tongues are a type of spiritual therapy for anxiety, turmoil, and perplexity. Paul wrote,

> *Do not be anxious about anything, but in everything, by prayer and petition, with thanksgiving, present your requests to God. And the peace of God, which transcends all understanding, will guard your hearts and your minds in Christ Jesus.*
> (Philippians 4:6–7 NIV)

9. TO HELP US IN GIVING THANKS

Tongues help those who are unlearned in spiritual things—and all of us, in fact—to offer the kind of thanks and praise to the King that He deserves. A combination of praying in human and spiritual language helps our minds and spirits to express our gratitude, in addition to other communication, to the King. Paul wrote, *"I will pray with my spirit, but I will also pray with my mind; I will sing with my spirit, but I will also sing with my mind"* (1 Corinthians 14:15 NIV).

10. TO BRING THE TONGUE UNDER SUBJECTION

Last—but not least—speaking in heaven-given languages places our tongues under the control of the Spirit of God, something that is much needed in all of our lives. We read in the New Testament book of James, *"But no man can tame the tongue. It is a restless evil, full of deadly poison.... Out of the same mouth come praise and cursing. My brothers, this should not be. Can both fresh water and salt water flow from the same spring?"* (James 3:8, 10–11 NIV). Only as the tongue is yielded to the Governor can it be controlled to speak words of life in keeping with the King and His kingdom.

I want to emphasize that speaking in tongues does not "belong" to charismatic or Pentecostal Christians. It is meant for the whole world because it is a gift the King-Son came to provide for all the inhabitants of the earth. It is intended for the seven billion people on earth right now. It is meant for all ethnic groups— Chinese, French, Sudanese, Australians, Danes, Mexicans—no one is excluded from God's intentions.

DAY 8

THE GIFT OF TONGUES

LESTER SUMRALL

God has set some in the church, first apostles, secondarily prophets, thirdly teachers, after that miracles, then gifts of healings, helps, governments, diversities of tongues.
—1 Corinthians 12:28

Diversities of tongues," or various kinds of tongues, is a gift used for public ministry. It is a sign gift from God, a distinguishing gift that does something very particular.

> *Wherefore tongues are for a sign, not to them that believe, but to them that believe not: but prophesying serves not for them that believe not, but for them which believe.*
>
> (1 Corinthians 14:22)

The gift of tongues is for a sign to the unbeliever, to stir him inside.

Speaking with tongues as the Holy Spirit gives utterance is a unique ministry that has not been used in other dispensations. It is identified only with the church age, the age we are living in today.

The phenomenon of speaking in tongues began on the day of Pentecost—the day the New Testament church was born in Jerusalem. This gift of tongues has been identified with the church since its inception, and it has not left the church since that day. None of the nine gifts has left the church.

This sign gift of various kinds of tongues is a supernatural utterance that comes from God through the person of the Holy Spirit. This remarkable gift is directed through man's spirit and manifests as a spirit language, a divine and spiritual communication that is different from his native tongue.

Tongues is the most misunderstood of all the spiritual gifts. There is no gift in the entire world that receives so explosive a reaction as the gift of tongues. Because the devil is afraid of it, he gets everybody fighting over it. If tongues did not cause him trouble, he would ignore it, but speaking in tongues is dynamic. It will change a person's life, so Satan fights it with every force he can muster. We need to understand it better so we can use it more. If we are going to use the sword, we must use it with dexterity. If we are going to use this gift of tongues, we must use it mightily as unto the Lord.

The sign gift of tongues is *not* the prayer language of tongues that comes with the infilling of the Holy Spirit. It is not the receiving of the Spirit at baptism when one is "filled with the Spirit," as in Acts 2:4: *"And they were all filled with the Holy Ghost, and began to speak with other tongues, as the Spirit gave them utterance."*

The gift of tongues is not the learning of foreign languages. Tongues has positively no relationship to the thinking abilities of man. When a person speaks in tongues, he has no understanding of what he is saying. The apostle Paul wrote, *"For if I pray in an unknown tongue, my spirit prays, but my understanding is unfruitful"* (1 Corinthians 14:14). His spirit is speaking to God. *"He that speaks in an unknown tongue speaks not to men, but to God"* (verse 2). Tongues is speech to God—a vocal miracle. What a joy it is to speak personally and directly to the Most High God!

This means there is an element of faith and an element of courage related to this gift. You must be able to say in faith, "Lord, I believe this is You." You must be able to say with courage, "I don't care what men think; I'm going to let the blessing of God flow through me."

God wants it to flow through each one of us. The gift of tongues is a special challenge and a sign to those, the Bible says, who are uninformed.

Only Spirit-filled, or Spirit-baptized, believers are candidates for this gift. The infilling of the Holy Spirit is the door to the operation of spiritual gifts in your life. You must pass through that door to reach all the "goodies" inside. Many people want these mighty gifts of the Spirit to function in their lives, but they are unwilling to step through that door.

Tongues is a part of the Great Commission to the church—the Lord Jesus Christ's last words on earth before He was taken up into heaven:

> *And He said to them, Go you into all the world, and preach the gospel to every creature. He that believes and is baptized shall be saved: but he that believes not shall be damned. And these signs shall follow them that believe; In My name shall they cast out devils; they shall speak with new tongues.*
> (Mark 16:15–17)

This gift was prophesied even by such a great Prophet as the Lord Jesus Christ. There is no doubt or ambiguity about what Jesus said. He said exactly what He meant and meant exactly what He said! It is available to each of us.

DAY 9

ON THE HOLY SPIRIT

JOHN WESLEY

*Even to this day, when Moses is read, the vail is upon their
heart. Nevertheless when he shall turn to the Lord, the vail
shall be taken away. Now the Lord is that Spirit: and where
the Spirit of the Lord is, there is liberty.*
—2 Corinthians 3:15–17

The apostle had been showing how the gospel ministry was superior to that of the law: The time being now come when types and
shadows should be laid aside, and we should be invited to our duty
by the manly and ingenuous motives of a clear and full revelation,
open and free on God's part, and not at all disguised by his ambas-
sadors. But what he chiefly insists upon is, not the manner, but the
subject of their ministry: *"Who also has made us able ministers,"*
saith he, *"of the new testament; not of the letter, but of the Spirit: for
the letter kills, but the Spirit gives life"* (verse 6). Here lies the great
difference between the two dispensations: That the law was indeed
spiritual in its demands, requiring a life consecrated to God in the
observance of many rules; but, not conveying spiritual assistance,

its effect was only to kill and mortify man, by giving him to understand, that he must needs be in a state of great depravity, since he found it so difficult to obey God; and that, as particular deaths were by that institution inflicted for particular sins, so death, in general, was but the consequence of his universal sinfulness. But the ministration of the New Testament was that of a "Spirit which gives life;"—a Spirit, not only promised, but actually conferred; which should both enable Christians now to live unto God, and fulfill precepts even more spiritual than the former; and restore them hereafter to perfect life, after the ruins of sin and death. The incarnation, preaching, and death of Jesus Christ were designed to represent, proclaim, and purchase for us this gift of the Spirit; and therefore says the apostle, "*The Lord is that Spirit*," or the Spirit.

This description of Christ was a proper inducement to Jews to believe on him; and it is still a necessary instruction to Christians, to regulate their expectations from him. But [we] think this age has made it particularly necessary to be well assured what Christ is to us: When that question is so differently resolved by the pious but weak accounts of some pretenders to faith on one hand, and by the clearer, but not perfectly Christian, accounts of some pretenders to reason on the other: While some derive from him a "righteousness of God," but in a sense somewhat improper and figurative; and others no more than a charter of pardon, and a system of morality: While some so interpret the gospel, as to place the holiness they are to be saved by in something divine, but exterior to themselves; and others, so as to place it in things really within themselves, but not more than human. Now, the proper cure of what indistinctness there is one way, and what infidelity in the other, seems to be contained in the doctrine of my text: "*The Lord is that Spirit*."

Well may a man ask his own heart, whether it is able to admit the Spirit of God. For where that divine Guest enters, the laws of another world must be observed: The body must be given up to martyrdom, or spent in the Christian warfare, as unconcernedly as if the soul were already provided of its house from heaven; the goods of this world must be parted with as freely, as if the last fire were to seize them tomorrow; our neighbor must be loved as heartily as if he were washed from all his sins, and demonstrated to be a child of God by the resurrection from the dead. The fruits of this Spirit must not be mere moral virtues, calculated for the comfort and decency of the present life; but holy dispositions, suitable to the instincts of a superior life already begun.

Thus to press forward, whither the promise of life calls him,— to turn his back upon the world, and comfort himself in God,— every one that has faith perceives to be just and necessary, and forces himself to do it: Every one that has hope, does it gladly and eagerly, though not without difficulty; but he that has love does it with ease and singleness of heart.

Let a man descend calmly into his heart, and see if there be no root of bitterness springing up; whether, at least, his thoughts, which are ever in motion, do not sometimes sally out into projects suggested by pride, or sink into indolent trifling, or be entangled in mean anxiety. Does not he find a motion of anger, or of gaiety, leavening him in an instant throughout; depriving him of the meekness and steady discernment he labored after? Or, let him but conceive at any time, that unfeigned obedience, and watchful zeal, and dignity of behavior, which, is suitable, I do not say to an angel, but to a sinner that has "a good hope through grace," and endeavor to work himself up to it; and if he find no sort of obstacle to this within him, he has indeed then no opportunity of suffering. In short, if he is such an abject sort of creature, as will, unless grace should do him a perpetual violence, relapse frequently into a course of thinking and acting entirely without God; then he can never want occasions of suffering, but will find his own nature to be the same burden to him, as that *faithless and perverse generation* was to our Savior, of whom he said, *"How long shall I be with you? how long shall I suffer you?"* (Matthew 17:17).

I will conclude all with that excellent Collect of our Church:—"O God, who in all ages hast taught the hearts of Thy faithful people, by sending to them the light of Thy Holy Spirit; grant us by the same Spirit to have a right judgment in all things, and evermore to rejoice in His holy comfort, through the merits of Jesus Christ our Savior; who lives and reigns with Thee, in the unity of the same Spirit, one God, world without end. Amen."

DAY 10

THE RIVER, THE WAVES, AND THE FLOW OF THE SPIRIT

GUILLERMO MALDONADO

Again he measured a thousand, and brought me through the waters; the waters were to the knees. Again he measured a thousand, and brought me through; the waters were to the loins. Afterward he measured a thousand; and it was a river that I could not pass over: for the waters were risen, waters to swim in, a river that could not be passed over.
—Ezekiel 47:4–5

As the body of Christ, the church is entering one of the most beautiful times of its history—the greatest outpouring of the Holy Spirit that the earth has ever seen, in preparation for Christ's return. It is important for us to recognize the trends and patterns that will lead us to grow and to flow correctly with this great spiritual revival. The Holy Spirit is the expression of God on the earth, and without Him we cannot know what operations the Lord is initiating or where He is leading us. If we want to experience the movements of God, we need to hear what the Spirit is saying in the now. (See, for example, Revelation 2:7.) We must be aware of how the Holy Spirit flows today, both in the church and throughout the rest of the earth.

In the recorded vision of the prophet Ezekiel above, the Holy Spirit is like the water in a river that eventually covers us as we enter deeper and deeper into it, until the only way across is to swim. That is how our relationship with Him should be; we must be completely submerged in His power, presence, and manifestation, until we can swim in the river of His presence and follow each new wave and movement that He brings to the earth. But we must understand the river, the waves, and the flow of the Holy Spirit.

"And he showed me a pure river of water of life, clear as crystal, proceeding from the throne of God and of the Lamb" (Revelation 22:1). The river of the Spirit carries activity from the throne of God to the earth and flows back to it. Those who are spiritually near the throne of God and know what the Spirit is saying today can understand the activity of the river. If we do not know the throne or the river that flows from it, the movements of the Holy Spirit will not make sense to us. The work of the Spirit of God will go over our heads because it does not fit in with our personal agendas.

Pastors and other leaders, if you believe it is hard for people to receive the river of the Holy Spirit through the assignment God has given to you, you need to radically change your way of thinking. Revival *is* coming to various cities of the United States, Europe, Africa, Latin America, and the rest of the world. There are prophetic streams, rivers of holiness, deliverance, prosperity, healings, miracles, and creative miracles flowing from the throne of God, and the Spirit is waiting for you to open the door and allow His river to flow through your territory. Whenever I go to another church to minister, I make sure that the pastors have received the spirit of revival, because if they have not, it will be impossible for the movement of the Spirit to continue there. Remember that every pastor is the door of their church; they are the person who either allows or stops that which comes from God. For this reason, revival must begin in the life of the pastor; otherwise, they will close the door on the flow of the Holy Spirit.

Sometimes people try to clone revivals that have occurred in other times or places, but they lack the true movement of the Spirit. It is possible to copy the forms of God, the way things have been done before, but the movement of the Spirit of God can never be cloned because the Holy Spirit has something different for each time, country, region, and believer. We need to discern the movements that the Lord has for our life and area and then become part of them in order to carry them in our spirit to share with others. The movements of the Spirit can only be felt or discerned when we participate in them.

For the Spirit's river to manifest, the *logos* and the *rhema* must work together. The *logos* is the written Word, inspired by the Holy Spirit, that establishes the doctrine of our faith; but what is written remains inert until it is revealed to us through a *rhema* word. A *rhema* is a spoken word of God for today, for a specific situation; it is the *logos* revealed in the now. The *logos* is the basis upon which the river of the Holy Spirit is established, and the *rhema* is what carries the movements of the Spirit. Every movement of the Spirit begins with a *rhema* based on the *logos*.

Do you want to participate in the next revival on earth? Enter the river of the Spirit that is flowing in the now. There is no excuse for us not to allow the Spirit to move in our lives and ministries.

DAY 11

THE COMING OF THE HOLY SPIRIT

AIMEE SEMPLE MCPHERSON

*"But Peter, standing up… said to them,…These are not
drunken, as you suppose, seeing it is but the third hour of the
day. But this is that which was spoken by the prophet Joel.
And it shall come to pass in the last days, says God, that I
will pour out of My Spirit upon all flesh.*
—Acts 2:14–17

And *when the day of Pentecost was fully come they were all with one
accord in one place. And suddenly there came a sound from heaven"*
(and bless God, there has been a sound ever since when the Spirit
falls and comes in). *"From heaven…"*—yes, thank God, in spite of
what man may say, undoubtedly this sound is from heaven. *"As of a
rushing mighty wind, and it filled all the house where they were sitting.
And there appeared to them cloven tongues like as of fire, and it sat
upon each of them. And they were all filled with the Holy Ghost, and
began to speak with other tongues, as the Spirit gave them utterance"*
(Acts 2:1–4).

I have often tried to picture the sudden consternation and excitement which surged through the streets of Jerusalem when the hundred and twenty men and women were filled with the Holy Spirit, and burst out shouting and talking in other tongues, so filled that they acted like drunken people. (See Acts 2:13.) I can seem to see the crowds running up this street and that, windows flying open, heads thrust out, doors opening, everybody running, devout men gathering up their long ministerial robes and forgetting their dignity, running with the rest to swell the one great question: *What means this?* (verse 12).

"*Now when this was noised abroad, the multitude came together* [beloved, if the Holy Spirit is falling in your midst, you will not need oyster suppers or box socials or Christmas trees to bring the multitude, your only trouble will be to find seats for the people] *and were confounded* [just as you have been, perhaps], *because that every man heard them speak in his own language*" (verse 6). They were amazed, they marveled, they were in doubt. Sober-minded folk asked the question: "*What means this?*"

Mockers declared, "*These men are full of new wine*" (verse 13). O, what an uproar! What an excitement! You dear people who dislike confusion and demand things to be done "decently and in order" would have been scandalized.

"*But Peter* [a new Peter, no longer afraid of the opinions of people], *standing up* [the Holy Spirit, when He endues you with power, puts a real 'stand up for Jesus spirit' within you, and removes your cowardice]... *said to them,...These are not drunken, as you suppose, seeing it is but the third hour of the day. But this is that which was spoken by the prophet Joel. And it shall come to pass in the last days, says God, that I will pour out of My Spirit upon all flesh*" (Acts 2:14–17). Then, as Peter preached that mighty sermon under the power of the Holy Spirit, among other things, he told his vast audience to:

"*Repent and be baptized, every one of you in the name of Jesus Christ for the remission of sins,*" and that they, too, would "*receive the gift of the Holy Spirit*" (Acts 2:38). Furthermore, just as though he looked away ahead through the coming years and saw the doubts in some of your minds, Peter declared that "*the promise is*" not only "*to you*" but also "*to your children, and to all that are afar off* [that means you, brother and sister, for he goes on to say], *even as many as the Lord our God shall call*" (verse 39). Now, if God has called you, the promise is to you. How glad I am that the Spirit, through Peter, drove these nails and clinched them on the other side until there is not the shadow of a loophole for you to thrust the wedge of doubt into.

DAY 12

GOD'S "I WILL"

REINHARD BONNKE

I will pray the Father, and He shall give you another
Comforter, that He may abide with you for ever.
—John 14:16

When God says, "I will," He forms a covenant. *"Because He could swear by no greater, He swore by Himself"* (Hebrews 6:13) to perform certain deeds. Usually, these covenants are unconditional, but some will fail if we do not grab hold of them and act upon them. We can describe this with the word *unilateral,* which refers to action by one party only. Genesis 9:8–10 gives us an example:

> *And God spoke to Noah, and to his sons with him, saying, And I, behold, I establish My covenant with you, and with your seed after you; and with every living creature that is with you, of the fowl, of the cattle, and of every beast of the earth with you; from all that go out of the ark, to every beast of the earth.*

This is a solo resolution, without a second party. It is unilateral. Nevertheless, it is for a second party. It is made for Noah, his sons, his descendants, and even for the birds and wild creatures that could not make any agreement with God. It contains no proviso and lays down no terms.

It is important to see that God's "I will" covenants have two qualities. They are spontaneous and they are absolute. Nobody pressed God for the covenants, and they stand firm without any condition. They are a sheer act of grace and concern from start to finish. That is, God and Jesus said, *"Have faith in God"* (Mark 11:22)—leave things to Him. He does all things well.

The Gospel of Matthew records thirteen undertakings of Christ using the words *"I will."* These thirteen are not the full complement of what He will do, but He speaks in the same way as the Lord God of the prophets, and He stands as the Son, by the side of His Father, as the great *"I will."*

Most of Christ's claims relate to the immediate present, not some far off future. He said:

Come to Me…and I will give you rest.   (Matthew 11:28)

Him that comes to Me I will in no wise cast out.
(John 6:37)

I will make you fishers of men.   (Matthew 4:19)

Each of these is backed by His truthfulness alone. Jesus never tries to convince people of what He has said. He does not argue. His words are enough, and if believed, they prove themselves. There is no other proof needed.

Behold My Servant, whom I uphold…. He shall not cry, nor lift up, nor cause His voice to be heard in the street…. He shall bring forth judgment to truth. He shall not fail nor be discouraged, till He have set judgment in the earth.

(Isaiah 42:1–4)

There is a tremendous *"I will"* in John 14:16. It is unconditional and inevitable, a sheer unsolicited act of the divine will. *"I will pray the Father, and He shall give you another Comforter, that He may abide with you for ever."* Christ did not say, "If you pray." He said, *"I will pray."* The disciples did not pray for it. The day of Pentecost was not the result of a church beseeching God and prevailing in perfect unity—as is so often suggested. It was the sovereign act of Christ and the Father independent of all human action.

It was also a fulfillment of the *"I will"* of God in Joel 2:28: *"I will pour out My Spirit upon all flesh."* God's outpoured Spirit is not a matter of the will of people and of their desires and prayers. The Helper has come.

The disciples were simply together on the day of Pentecost. They were not praying. They were sitting together for mutual support at a critical time. Then Jesus simply did what He said He would do. They did not ask Him to do it. There was no need. He said He would, and He did.

The Lord has also fulfilled His promise in the twentieth century. The major part of the churches, even the evangelicals, attempted to stop what was happening. Many of them had prayed for revival, but they opposed the form in which it came. But God had said He would pour out His Spirit, and nothing could stop Him. He has, and He continues to do so. Now a major section of the worldwide church has plunged into the river flowing from the throne.

Christ said, *"I will build My church."* He has, He still is doing so, and He will complete it. As believers, we are on the side of the inevitable. He walks with victory, and He faces the dawn, not the darkness. The kingdom is coming.

DAY 13

RECEIVE YE THE HOLY GHOST

WILLIAM SEYMOUR

Now He which stablishes us with you in Christ,
and has anointed us, is God, who has also sealed us,
and given the earnest of the Spirit in our hearts.
—2 Corinthians 1: 21–22

The first step in seeking the baptism with the Holy Ghost is to have a clear knowledge of the new birth in our souls, which is the first work of grace and brings everlasting life to our souls. *"Therefore being justified by faith, we have peace with God"* (Romans 5:1). Every one of us that repents of our sins and turns to the Lord Jesus with faith in Him, receives forgiveness of sins. Justification and regeneration are simultaneous. The pardoned sinner becomes a child of God in justification.

The next step for us is to have a clear knowledge, by the Holy Spirit, of the second work of grace wrought in our hearts by the power of the blood and the Holy Ghost. *"For by one offering, He has perfected for ever them that are sanctified. Whereof the Holy*

Ghost also is a witness to us" (Hebrews 10:14–15). The Scripture also teaches, "*For both He that sanctifies and they who are sanctified are all of one: for which cause He is not ashamed to call them brethren*" (Hebrews 2:11). So we have Christ crowned and enthroned in our heart, "the tree of life." We have the brooks and streams of salvation flowing in our souls, but, praise God, we can have the rivers. For the Lord Jesus says, "*He that believes on Me, as the scripture has said, out of his belly shall flow rivers of living water. This spoke He of the Spirit…for the Holy Ghost was not yet given*" (John 7:38–39). But, praise our God, He is now given and being poured out on all flesh. All races, nations, and tongues are receiving the baptism with the Holy Ghost and fire, according to the prophecy of Joel.

When we have a clear knowledge of justification and sanctification, through the precious blood of Jesus Christ in our hearts, then we can be a recipient of the baptism with the Holy Ghost. Many people today are sanctified, cleansed from all sin, and perfectly consecrated to God, but they have never obeyed the Lord according to Acts 1, 4, 5, 8 and Luke 24:39, for their real personal Pentecost, the enduement of power for service and work and for sealing unto the day of redemption. The baptism with the Holy Ghost is a free gift without repentance upon the sanctified, cleansed vessel. "*Now He which stablishes us with you in Christ, and has anointed us, is God, who has also sealed us, and given the earnest of the Spirit in our hearts*" (2 Corinthians 1:21–22). I praise our God for the sealing of the Holy Spirit unto the day of redemption.

Dearly beloved, the only people that will meet our Lord and Savior Jesus Christ and go with Him into the marriage supper of the Lamb, are the wise virgins—not only saved and sanctified, with pure and clean hearts, but also having the baptism with the Holy Ghost. The others we find will not be prepared. They have some oil in their lamps but they have not the double portion of His Spirit.

Before Pentecost, the disciples were filled with the unction of the Holy Spirit that sustained them until they received the Holy Ghost baptism. Many people today are filled with joy and gladness, but they are far from the enduing of power. Sanctification brings rest and sweetness and quietness to our souls, for we are one with the Lord Jesus and are able to obey His precious Word, that *"man shall not live by bread alone but by every word that proceeds out of the mouth of God"* (Matthew 4:4), and we are feeding upon Christ. But let us wait for the promise of the Father upon our souls, according to Jesus's word: *"John truly baptized with water; but you shall be baptized with the Holy Ghost not many days from now. …You shall receive power, after that the Holy Ghost is come upon you: and you shall be witnesses to Me, both in Jerusalem and in all Judea, and in Samaria, and to the uttermost part of the earth"* (Acts 1:5, 8). Glory! Glory! Hallelujah! O worship, get down on your knees and ask the Holy Ghost to come in, and you will find Him right at your heart's door, and He will come in. Prove Him now. Amen.

DAY 14

OUR HEARTS, HIS DWELLING PLACE

D. L. MOODY

*Even the Spirit of truth; whom the world cannot receive,
because it sees Him not, neither knows Him: but you know
Him; for He dwells with you, and shall be in you.*
—John 14:17

I firmly believe that the moment our hearts are emptied of selfishness and ambition and selfseeking and everything that is contrary to God's law, the Holy Spirit will come and fill every corner of our hearts; but if we are full of pride and conceit, ambition and self-seeking, pleasure and the world, there is no room for the Spirit of God. I also believe that many a man is praying to God to fill him, when he is full already with something else. Before we pray that God would fill us, I believe we ought to pray that He would empty us.

There must be an emptying before there can be a filling; and when the heart is turned upside down, and everything that is contrary to God is turned out, then the Spirit will come, just as

He did in the tabernacle, and fill us with His glory. We read in 2 Chronicles 5:13–14:

> *It came even to pass, as the trumpeters and singers were as one, to make one sound to be heard in praising and thanking the* Lord; *and when they lifted up their voice with the trumpets and cymbals and instruments of music, and praised the* Lord, *saying, For He is good; for His mercy endures for ever: that then the house was filled with a cloud, even the house of the* Lord; *so that the priests could not stand to minister by reason of the cloud: for the glory of the* Lord *had filled the house of God.*

We find in the Scriptures that, at the very moment that Solomon completed the temple, when all was finished, the people were praising God with one heart. The choristers and the singers and the ministers were all one; there was not any discord. They were all praising God, and the glory of God came and just filled the temple as a dwelling place. Now, as you turn over into the New Testament, you will find that believers, instead of tabernacles and temples, are now the dwelling place of the Holy Spirit. (See John 14:17.)

On the Day of Pentecost, before Peter preached that memorable sermon, the Holy Spirit came as they were praying, and He came in mighty power. We pray now for the Spirit of God to come, and we sing:

Come, Holy Spirit, heavenly dove,
    With all thy quickening power;
Kindle a flame of heavenly love
    In these cold hearts of ours.

I believe that it is perfectly right for us to pray in this way, if we understand it; but if we are praying for Him to come out of heaven and down to earth again, that is wrong, because He is already here. The Holy Spirit has not been absent from this earth for nineteen hundred years; He has been in the church, and He is with all believers. The believers in the church are the calledout ones; they are called out from the world, and every true believer is a temple for the Holy Spirit to dwell in.

"Greater is He that is in you, than he that is in the world" (1 John 4:4). If we have the Spirit dwelling in us, He gives us power over the flesh and the world, and over every enemy. *"He dwells with you, and shall be in you."*

There were some men burying an aged saint some time ago, and he was very poor, like many of God's people: they are poor in this world, but they are very rich; they have all the riches on the other side of life; they have laid up their riches where thieves cannot get them, and where swindlers cannot take them away from them, and where moths cannot corrupt them. (See Matthew 6:19–20.) This aged man, likewise, was very rich in the other world, and they were just hastening him off to the grave, wanting to get rid of him, when an old minister who was officiating at the grave said, "Tread softly, for you are carrying the temple of the Holy Ghost."

Whenever you see a believer, you see a temple of the Holy Spirit.

In 1 Corinthians 6:19–20, we read again:

Know you not that your body is the temple of the Holy Ghost which is in you, which you have of God, and you are not your own? For you are bought with a price: therefore glorify God in your body, and in your spirit, which are God's.

Thus are we taught that there is a divine resident in every child of God.

I think it is clearly taught in the Scriptures that every believer has the Holy Spirit dwelling in him. He may be quenching the Spirit of God, and he may not glorify God as he should, but if he is a believer in the Lord Jesus Christ, the Holy Spirit dwells in him.

DAY 15

SUPERNATURAL INVASION

KYNAN BRIDGES

Knowing the time, that now it is high time to awake out of sleep: for now is our salvation nearer than when we believed.
—Romans 13:11

The Bible says it is high time to wake up! The church of Christ is in need of a spiritual awakening, and that will happen only by way of a supernatural "invasion" *of* and *from* heaven. I believe we are on the brink of the greatest move of the Spirit of God this generation has ever seen. This shift is not only going to take place on a collective level, but also on an individual level. Many believers are already beginning to experience the shift. Perhaps something is stirring inside you that you have not been able to explain. There has been a godly discontentment within you that you have not fully understood.

There is no better time than the present to accommodate God moving in our midst. Right now is the *kairos* moment, the "high time" for magnificent divine movements to take place, when God interrupts the natural course of events with supernatural break-throughs. Our part is to ensure that we are always in position, ready for Him to work in and through us.

In John 5:1–9, there is an account of a man at the Pool of Bethesda whose story illustrates many spiritual truths. This man was an invalid and in a terrible condition physically, but he also had deep spiritual needs, and Jesus singled him out for a miracle. The aspects of this story I especially want to emphasize are the commands Jesus gave the man as He healed him: *"rise," "take up your bed,"* and *"walk."* (See verse 8.) One time, after reading this passage in John, I began to do a word study on those three commands. The Greek word translated *"rise"* means "to waken," or "to rouse"—as when you wake someone up who is sleeping, for example.

This man wasn't asleep physically, but he was asleep spiritually. He was asleep to the things of God. He was asleep to his destiny. He was asleep to his identity. He was asleep to his purpose, potential, and assignment from God. Then Jesus came and told him, *"Rise"*! Essentially, Jesus was releasing this man from his bondage by getting him to change his position.

Second, Jesus told him, *"Take up your bed."* This was a change of environment. He would no longer have to be bedridden; he was empowered to take responsibility for his life and destiny.

There was a time in my life when I lived like the man at the Pool of Bethesda. I didn't know what I was doing or where I was going. I was frustrated that I couldn't seem to experience prosperity in my life. This required a radical shift in my attitude. I had to allow the Holy Spirit to challenge many of my false notions. I had to admit that my approach was wrong. It wasn't that God hadn't blessed me—it was that I had not *received*.

Last, Jesus told the man to *"walk."* The original Greek term means, among other things, "to make due use of opportunities"— which would enable him to prosper in his purpose and assignment.

In other words, because of his incapacitation, the man had not been able to see or participate in divine opportunities. Opportunities had been passing him by that he hadn't recognized because of the state of spiritual slumber he had been in.

For the same reason, I believe the church is in need of spiritual awakening. The Lord is working in the earth, but many believers are asleep to His activities; they don't realize the ways in which He is moving. Yet, while they are asleep to these spiritual realities, they are often alert to temporal pursuits. It's easy for us to focus our attention and excitement on pastimes like entertainment, politics, sports, and so on, but when it comes to spiritual matters, we suddenly get bored and are easily distracted.

Many of us need to "unplug" from our diversions and distractions so we can hear what God is saying. When our time of visitation comes, we can't be looking the other way. God wants us to come out of all forms of spiritual slumber and have our senses awakened to supernatural realities.

God is saying, "It's time for you to wake up!" *"Awake you that sleep, and arise from the dead, and Christ shall give you light"* (Ephesians 5:14). This is not the time to go to sleep—or stay asleep. It's the time to watch. Remember, in the garden of Gethsemane, Jesus asked His disciples to watch with Him as He prayed. But they were sleeping during the time of watching. (See Mark 14:32–38.) Don't sleep during your season of visitation!

This is the time for the church to be awakened to the things of the Spirit. This is the time for the church to arise. Let's wake up and get excited about God, because this is our moment!

DAY 16

THE SPIRIT REVEALS THE DEEP THINGS OF GOD

MARIA WOODWORTH-ETTER

*Eye has not seen, nor ear heard, neither have entered into the
heart of man, the things which God has prepared for them
that love Him. But God has revealed them to us
by His Spirit: for the Spirit searches all things,
yea, the deep things of God.*
—1 Corinthians 2:9–10

This passage is not understood by anyone unless he has the Holy
Spirit. Many people today apply this to eternity, to the other world;
they think that we never know these things until we get into the
other world. I am glad that the Scripture explains itself. *"Eye has
not seen"*—in the natural state. God has, in the present, revealed
things to us by His Spirit, by His Spirit in this world. *"The Spirit
searches all things, yea, the deep things of God."*

I desire to especially call your attention to verse 14: *"The natural man receives not the things of the Spirit of God: for they are foolishness to him: neither can he know them, because they are spiritually
discerned."*

The natural man cannot understand this wonderful Scripture. There are two classes of men: the spiritual man and the natural man. The natural man is *"in the gall of bitterness, and in the bond of iniquity"* (Acts 8:23); the spiritual man is *"born of God"* (1 John 3:9) and walks in the Spirit; he gets out into the deep. The natural man can never discern spiritual things; he can never hear and understand the work of the Lord. These things pass all human understanding. The wisdom of this world, intellect, and science can never understand the spiritual things of God.

There are two kinds of wisdom. *"The wisdom of this world is foolishness with God"* (1 Corinthians 3:19). The natural man cannot comprehend the wisdom from above. (See James 3:17.) It never enters his imagination to think of the things God has prepared for those who love Him. He has prepared them already, and He has revealed them to us by His Spirit. His Spirit lets us down into the deep things, even the *"deep things of God."* This is what we preach, what we practice, and what we stand on. The work of the Spirit is foolishness to the natural man; but he who has the Spirit can discern spiritual things.

There are many kinds of power and many spirits going out in the world today. We are told to *"try the spirits"* (1 John 4:1); they are many. Everything is revealed by God through the blessed Holy Spirit. There is only one Spirit that we want anything to do with: not our own spirits, or any other spirit, but the Spirit of the living God. *"As many as are led by the Spirit of God, they are the sons of God"* (Romans 8:14).

The Spirit will lead us into all truth, all the way. He will lead us where we can get the truth. The child of God will be led into the baptism of the Holy Spirit and of fire (see Matthew 3:11), the Pentecostal baptism. Then we can go from one deep thing to another. The Holy Spirit is sent to us by Jesus Christ, and all gifts come through the Holy Spirit. Jesus said of the Spirit, *"He shall not speak of Himself; but whatsoever He shall hear, that shall He speak: and He will show you things to come. He shall glorify Me"* (John 16:13–14). We believe it. Glory to God!

This is the Holy Spirit who came at Pentecost and turned Jerusalem upside down. Jesus said that when the Holy Spirit came, He would abide with us forever (see John 14:16), even unto the end. The work of the Spirit is foolishness to the natural man; he cannot comprehend it.

Unless you will hear the voice of God, the voice of the natural man will make you attribute what you see to excitement or to some other power. When the Holy Spirit is poured out, two kinds of people are revealed: one is convinced and convicted, and accepts it; the other says, "If I accept this, I will have to lead a different life and be a laughingstock for the world." They are not willing to pay the price, so they begin to draw back. At first they are amazed at the strange works of God. Then, when they won't accept them, they begin to despise them. Everyone who continues to despise the works of the Holy Spirit will perish.

The Lamb of God left the realm of glory and came down here to be footsore, dusty, weary, and spit upon. He said, "*I come to do Your will, O God*" (Hebrews 10:9). If He had not borne all these things, if He had not gone all the way to the cross, the Holy Spirit never could have come. If Jesus had been left in the tomb, the Holy Spirit never could have come. As soon as He arose from the dead and ascended into heaven, the Holy Spirit could come.

God gave His Son the highest place, before all the hosts of heaven. Then He sent the Holy Spirit to dwell in these bodies of ours, His temple. (See 1 Corinthians 3:16.) The Spirit was to be given after Jesus was glorified. The Holy Spirit is a great power. In the Bible, He is compared to wind, water, and fire.

At Pentecost, He came like a cyclone, a "*rushing mighty wind*" (Acts 2:2). He comes like "*rivers of living water*" (John 7:38). He comes like fire; tongues of fire sat upon each of the disciples at Pentecost. (See Acts 2:1–4.) Wind, water, and fire—the most destructive elements we have, yet the most useful. God uses these images to denote the mighty power of the Holy Spirit.

DAY 17

HELP IS ON ITS WAY!

CAROL MCLEOD

But you shall receive power, after that the Holy Ghost is come upon you: and you shall be witnesses to Me both in Jerusalem, and in all Judaea, and in Samaria, and to the uttermost part of the earth.
—Acts 1:8

The Greek word translated *"power"* in this verse is *dunamis*, from which we derive the English word *dynamite*. *Dunamis* can be translated as "explosive strength, ability, and power." The Holy Spirit is a Gift Giver extraordinaire, and He knows exactly what you need to make it through the storms of life.

As incredible as you are—because you have been made by God at this moment in history in order to live a significant and abundant life—you will be unable to accomplish anything at all without the Spirit's *dunamis* power. You have been especially created and redeemed to receive that power; *dunamis* is a perfect fit for your remarkable container.

The wonder of Acts 1:8 is found in the statements *"You shall receive..."* and *"You shall be...."* When you receive the power of the Holy Spirit, you become someone you could never be on your own. You need the power of the Spirit to enable you to walk in your calling and destiny in Christ. The Holy Spirit changes ordinary men and women into powerful witnesses for Christ and His kingdom. *Dunamis* changes wimps into witnesses and deniers into testifiers.

When Jesus was arrested by the authorities, all His disciples ran scared. (See Matthew 26:47–56; Mark 14:43–50.) After Jesus's arrest, Peter denied Him three times. (See, for example, Luke 22:55–62.) When Jesus was crucified, all the disciples except for John were absent. (See John 19:25–27.) Yet, after the Holy Spirit filled these fearful, intimidated men, it was said of them:

> *These that have turned the world upside down are come here also.* (Acts 17:6)

Jesus knew that we who live this side of heaven's peaceful shores would never outlast a storm without the *dunamis* power of the Holy Spirit!

> *When the day of Pentecost was fully come, they were all with one accord in one place. And suddenly there came a sound from heaven as of a rushing mighty wind, and it filled all the house where they were sitting. And there appeared to them cloven tongues like as of fire, and it sat upon each of them. And they were all filled with the Holy Ghost, and began to speak with other tongues, as the Spirit gave them utterance.* (Acts 2:1–4)

The power of Pentecost was never meant to be a one-time spiritual high but a new way of knowing God, living for God, serving God, and being filled with God!

Isn't it interesting that the sound of the Holy Spirit at Pentecost is described as *"a rushing mighty wind"*? That sound must have been tremendous! Although I have never heard the roar of a tornado, I have heard it likened to the sound of a fighter jet taking off or a huge freight train coming down the tracks. The mighty sound heard by the believers who were gathered in the upper room was loud enough, unusual enough, and perhaps terrifying enough that people in the surrounding area began to gather to find out what was going on.

The *dunamis* force of heaven had interrupted the disciples' formerly calm prayer meeting! The energy of heaven had broken loose around them, and the power of heaven was in their midst. They were walking in an atmosphere permeated with the courage and authority of heaven. If you are in a storm today, you desperately need your life to be invaded by this life-changing dynamism as well!

What happened next is the stuff of fantasy, but it is 100 percent historically accurate. The manifestation of the Holy Spirit not only sounded like a mighty, rushing wind, but it looked like fire. Luke described it as one hundred and twenty separate *"tongues like as of fire,"* which rested on each believer. Not one person was left out—everyone heard the sound of the wind and received a tongue of fire upon them. John the Baptist had announced that Jesus would baptize His followers *"with the Holy Ghost and with fire"* (see, for example, Luke 3:16), and this was the moment when that all began. *"And suddenly there came a sound from heaven as of a rushing mighty wind, and it filled all the house where they were sitting. And there appeared to them cloven tongues like as of fire...."* I know this to be a scientific fact: when wind meets fire, it is inevitable that the fire will spread! Always!

After the wind and the fire, the third tangible sign of the *dunamis* power of the Holy Spirit was that believers began to speak with other tongues as the Spirit gave them utterance. Now, let me challenge you—don't read this account only in a historical sense, as you may have read it hundreds of times previously. Read this account as if you were in that very room.

Even though the believers couldn't comprehend what the Holy Spirit had given them to speak, the words had meaning for the God-fearing Jews who had come from many countries and regions to worship in Jerusalem and were now gathered to listen to these extraordinary *"tongues"* that told—in their own languages—of *"the wonders of God."* (See Acts 2:5–11 NIV.)

As far as we know, Jesus never spoke in a language that He didn't learn from His earthly parents or from a teacher. The disciples did, however, because this was the very first example of the *"greater works"* that Jesus said His disciples would accomplish. (See John 14:12.) At Pentecost, we also see the fulfillment of the words of Jesus when He promised, "The Holy Spirit is with you but will be in you" (see John 14:17), and *"When the Helper comes, whom I shall send to you from the Father, the Spirit of truth who proceeds from the Father, He will testify of Me"* (John 15:26 NKJV).

We all need help, don't we? The help that we have been given to live a powerful and creative life this side of heaven is found in the Person of the Holy Spirit!

DAY 18

THE HOLY SPIRIT POURED OUT AT PENTECOST

MYLES MUNROE

This Jesus has God raised up, whereof we all are witnesses.
Therefore being by the right hand of God exalted, and having
received of the Father the promise of the Holy Ghost, He has
shed forth this, which you now see and hear.
—Acts 2:32–33

After Jesus ascended to heaven, His disciples, along with over one hundred other followers, met together and awaited the coming of the Governor of God's kingdom on earth [the Holy Spirit]. His arrival occurred on the day of Pentecost, which means "fiftieth" in Greek. Pentecost was a harvest feast held on the fiftieth day after the Passover feast. Jesus appeared to His followers over a period of forty days after His resurrection, and they waited ten days from His ascension for the coming of the Spirit.

When the day of Pentecost was fully come, they were all
together in one place. And suddenly there came a sound from
heaven as of a rushing mighty wind, and it filled all the house

where they were sitting. And there appeared to them cloven tongues like as of fire, and it sat upon each of them. And they were filled with the Holy Ghost, and began to speak in other tongues [languages], as the Spirit gave them utterance.

(Acts 2:1–4)

When Jesus's followers were *filled* with the Holy Spirit, they were given power to speak in the variety of languages spoken by the Jewish people who had come to Jerusalem, from a number of countries, to celebrate the feast of Pentecost. (See Acts 2:5–11.) The heavenly government gave them the ability to communicate the message that the kingdom of God had fully come so that people of many nations could hear this momentous news. Their speaking in these languages was an evidence that they were connected to the King and their assignment to bring the kingdom of heaven to earth. As recorded in the book of Mark, Jesus had previously told his disciples, *"And these signs shall follow them that believe; in My name shall they…speak with new tongues…"* (Mark 16:17).

Luke reported that the people who heard them said, in essence, "Why are you speaking like this; what is going on with you?" The disciple Peter responded,

You men of Judaea, and all you that dwell at Jerusalem, be this known to you, and hearken to my words: For these are not drunken, as you suppose, seeing it is but the third hour of the day. But this is that which was spoken by the prophet Joel; And it shall come to pass in the last days, says God, I will pour out of My Spirit upon all flesh: and your sons and your daughters shall prophesy, and your young men shall see visions, and your old men shall dream dreams: and on My servants and on My handmaidens I will pour out in those days of My Spirit; and they shall prophesy.… This Jesus has God raised up, whereof we all are witnesses. Therefore being by the right hand of God exalted, and having received of the

Father [King] *the promise of the Holy Ghost* [Governor], *He*
has shed forth this, which you now see and hear.

(Acts 2:14–18, 32–33)

Once again, we see the promise of the Father announced; but
this time, the news was that the promise of the King was now fulfilled in the return of the Governor [the Holy Spirit]. Peter was
telling them they were witnessing the influence of the government
of heaven through the arrival of the Holy Spirit.

When Jesus's disciples received the Holy Spirit, and then were
filled by the Spirit when He was poured out at Pentecost, this sig-
naled a seismic change on earth. The way was now open, for all
people who received the cleansing Jesus provided, to receive the
presence and power of the Governor. What separates the kingdom
of heaven from all other philosophies, belief systems, and religions
is that its citizens have within them the Holy Spirit. Religions
have doctrines, tenets, and lists of *do*'s and *don't*s, but they don't
have the indwelling Spirit.

While the Holy Spirit once dwelled only in Jesus, now He
is able to dwell in millions of people throughout the world. He's
back home in the colony so that the whole planet can be filled with
the glory of the King. Now that He has been poured out, He can
be all over the world at the same time. He lives in people of all
races and skin colors. He lives in both men and women. The physical Jesus had only two hands with which to bless children and
break bread for the hungry and relieve the sick. Now, through the
Spirit dwelling in the lives of His followers, there are millions of
hands doing the work of the kingdom. While Jesus's ministry was
once limited to the area of Palestine, it can now be in Australia,
China, the United States, the Bahamas, and all over the world at
the same time. His purpose is to spread the kingdom of God on
earth through a multitude of people, in a multitude of ways, in all
spheres of life.

The power of the Governor is that He makes the reality of heaven on earth possible. This is why *everybody* needs the Holy Spirit. He is the only one who can connect us to the King and, through us, dispel the kingdom of darkness with His kingdom of light.

DAY 19

RECEIVING THE INBREATHED SPIRIT

DEREK PRINCE

*Then said Jesus to them again, Peace be to you:
as My Father has sent Me, even so send I you.
And when He had said this, He breathed on them,
and says to them, Receive you the Holy Ghost.*
—John 20:21–22

I want to discuss what it meant for Jesus's disciples to receive the inbreathed Spirit. The day Jesus was resurrected, He appeared to the disciples as a group.

Then the same day at evening, being the first day of the week, when the doors were shut where the disciples were assembled for fear of the Jews, came Jesus and stood in the midst, and says to them, Peace be to you. And when He had so said, He showed to them His hands and His side. (John 20:19–20)

Though His body had been wonderfully transformed, it still retained the visible marks of His crucifixion as indisputable evidence of the fact that He was the very same Person whom they had seen crucified and die on the cross. We read, *"Then were the disciples glad, when they saw the Lord"* (verse 20).

I am sure that tremendous, indescribable joy filled their hearts when they really grasped the fact that He was alive.

Then said Jesus to them again, Peace be to you: as My Father has sent Me, even so send I you. And when He had said this, He breathed on them, and says to them, Receive you the Holy Ghost. (verses 21–22)

"He breathed on them." The Greek word for *"breathed"* is used in secular Greek of a flute player breathing into the mouth of his flute to produce music. And a person who is playing a flute or any similar instrument does not stand at a distance and blow at it. He brings it right up to his mouth and fits his mouth to the mouthpiece and blows into it. Now, I cannot prove this, and I'm not attempting to, but to me the implication is that Jesus did not stand and breathe at the disciples in a group but came to each one individually and breathed into him.

I believe there is a great difference between the breath of life Adam received and the breath the disciples received. This was life that had triumphed over death. This was eternal life. Indestructible life. Life that neither sin, death, Satan, nor anything else could ever conquer or overcome. He breathed into them totally victorious life, His own life. And He said, *"Receive you the Holy Ghost."*

In the Greek, the definite article *the* is not there. Bear in mind that the word translated *"Ghost,"* which is *pneuma*, also means breath or wind. So we might legitimately translate this as, "Receive holy breath." I believe His action went with His words. He breathed into them holy breath, divine resurrection life breath, and they were created anew. This is the moment when the new creation took place for the first time.

The disciples received the Holy Spirit not primarily as a Person, but as breath, as divine resurrection eternal life. They received the resurrected Christ and the inbreathed Spirit. But the promises Jesus had given in John's gospel all the way through were not yet fulfilled.

The fact that the promise of the Holy Spirit had not yet been fulfilled is very important to understand because, forty days later, Jesus still referred to those promises as being in the future. We see this in the book of Acts, at the time just before Jesus ascended to heaven, when He told His disciples,

> *For John truly baptized with water; but you shall be baptized with the Holy Ghost not many days from now.*   (Acts 1:5)

> *But you shall receive power, after that the Holy Ghost is come upon you.*   (Acts 1:8)

Luke also recorded these instructions of Jesus to His disciples just before He ascended: *"Behold, I send the promise of My Father upon you: but tarry you in the city of Jerusalem, until you be endued with power from on high"* (Luke 24:49).

A little while later, Peter explained to the crowd that had gathered, *"This is what was spoken by the prophet Joel: 'And it shall come to pass in the last days, says God, I will pour out of My Spirit upon all flesh'"* (Acts 2:16–17). These words show us what we are dealing with here. This was the promise. Peter explained that the Holy Spirit was given because Jesus had been glorified.

> *This Jesus has God raised up, whereof we all are witnesses. Therefore being by the right hand of God exalted, and having received of the Father the promise of the Holy Ghost, He has shed forth this, which you now see and hear.* (Acts 2:32–33)

This was the culmination of all those promises. When Jesus was glorified in heaven, He received from the Father the promise of the Spirit and then poured out the Holy Spirit on the waiting disciples. What we are talking about in receiving the baptism in the Holy Spirit is the same experience the disciples received on the day of Pentecost.

DAY 20

BROKENNESS PRECEDES BLESSING

SMITH WIGGLESWORTH

*But what things were gain to me, those I counted loss for
Christ. Yea doubtless, and I count all things but loss for the
excellency of the knowledge of Christ Jesus my Lord:
for whom I have suffered the loss of all things, and do count
them but dung, that I may win Christ.*
—Philippians 3:7–8

We must acknowledge our helplessness and nothingness.
Although laboring in the Spirit is painful, God can lift the burden
from us. I have had those days when I feel burdened. And I say,
brother and sister, unless God brings us into a place of brokenness of spirit, unless God remolds us in the great plan of His will
for us, the best of us will utterly fail. But when we are absolutely
taken in hand by the Almighty, God turns even our weakness into
strength. He makes even that barren, helpless, groaning cry come
forth, so that men and women are reborn in the travail. There is a
place where our helplessness is touched by the power of God and

where we come out shining as *"gold tried in the fire"* (Revelation 3:18).

There is no hope for Pentecost unless we come to God in our brokenness. It was on the cross that our Lord died with a broken heart. Pentecost came out of jeering and sneering. It included being mocked and beaten and an offer of sour wine. He received an unfair judgment and a cross that He had to bear. But, glory to God, Pentecost rings out this morning for you through the words, *"It is finished!"* (John 19:30). And now because it is finished, we can take the same place that He took and rise out of that death in majestic glory with the resurrection touch of heaven. People will know that God has done something for us.

Daily, there must be a revival touch in our hearts. He must change us after His fashion. We are to be made new all the time. There is no such thing as having all grace and knowledge. God wants us to begin with these words of power found in Philippians 3 and never stop, but go on to perfection. God wants us to reach the blessings in these verses today:

Read Hebrews 10:32: *"But call to remembrance the former days, in which, after you were illuminated, you endured a great fight of afflictions."* I am positive that no man can attain like-mindedness except by the illumination of the Spirit.

God has been speaking to me over and over that I must urge people to receive the baptism of the Holy Spirit. In the baptism of the Holy Spirit, there is unlimited grace and endurance as the Spirit reveals Himself to us. The excellency of Christ can never be understood apart from illumination. And I find that the Holy Spirit is the great Illuminator who makes me understand all the depths of Him. I must witness about Christ. Jesus said to Thomas, *"Thomas, because you have seen Me, you have believed: blessed are they that have not seen, and yet have believed"* (John 20:29).

There is a revelation that brings us into touch with Him where we get all and see right into the fullness of Christ. As Paul saw the depths and heights of the grandeur, he longed that he might win Him. Before his conversion, in his passion and zeal, Paul would do anything to bring Christians to death. His passion raged like a mighty lion. As he was going to Damascus, he heard the voice of Jesus saying, *"Saul, Saul, why persecute you Me?"* (Acts 9:4). What touched him was the tenderness of God.

Friends, it is always God's tenderness that reaches us. He comes to us in spite of our weakness and depravity. If somebody came to oppose us, we would stand our ground, but when He comes to forgive us, we do not know what to do. Oh, to win Christ! A thousand things in the nucleus of a human heart need softening a thousand times a day. There are things in us that unless God shows us *"the excellency of the knowledge of Christ Jesus,"* we will never be broken and brought to ashes. But God will do it. We will not merely be saved, but we will be saved a thousand times over! Oh, this transforming regeneration by the power of the Spirit of the living God makes me see there is a place to *"win Christ,"* that I may stand complete there. As He was, so am I to be. The Scriptures declare that we can be:

> *Found in Him, not having [our] own righteousness, which is of the law, but that which is through the faith of Christ, the righteousness which is of God by faith.*   (Philippians 3:9)

We cannot depend upon our works, but upon the faithfulness of God, being able under all circumstances to be hidden in Him, covered by the almighty presence of God. The Scriptures tell us that we are in Christ and Christ is in God. What is able to move you from this place of omnipotent power? *"Shall tribulation, or distress, or persecution, or famine, or nakedness, or peril, or sword?"* (Romans 8:35). Oh, no! Will life, or death, or principalities, or powers? (See verse 38.) No, *"we are more than conquerors through Him that loved us"* (verse 37).

DAY 21

THE ANOINTING OF THE SPIRIT

JOSHUA MILLS

*Now thanks be to God, which always causes us to triumph in
Christ, and makes manifest the savor of His knowledge by us
in every place. For we are to God a sweet savor of Christ, in
them that are saved, and in them that perish.*
—2 Corinthians 2:14–15

In biblical times, shepherds smeared anointing oil over their sheep
to keep them from being bitten by annoying insects. During the
summer months, it was common for nasal flies to attack the heads
of the sheep, burrowing deep into their nose and even into their
brain. This could cause a severe infection, leading to irritation,
disease, or even death, as the sheep would often bash their heads
upon rocks and trees in an attempt to find relief from the pain
caused by the flies. To protect the sheep, the shepherd made a mix-
ture of olive oil, sulfur, and other spices. He used it to anoint his
sheep by smearing it across their foreheads and around their ears
and noses. This anointing brought total protection to the sheep.

As David so beautifully sang in his twenty-third psalm, *"You anoint my head with oil; my cup runs over"* (Psalm 23:5). This gives us an understanding that as the Spirit smears His anointing over us, He covers us with a supernatural protection against the attacks of the enemy that try to bring irritation, frustration, sickness, or even death. Being covered by His anointing gives us power over obstacles and the ability to overcome any problem that presents itself.

The anointing oil used to anoint sheep was also fragrant with spices:

> *For we are to God a sweet savor of Christ, in them that are saved, and in them that perish.*   (2 Corinthians 2:15)

As we are anointed, we become the fragrance.

In Old Testament times when the holy incense was burned in the temple in Jerusalem, the fragrance could be smelled all the way to Jericho, a distance of about sixteen miles. Isn't that amazing? The Spirit smears a fragrant anointing over your life that reaches unto heaven, but God is not the only one who smells it. It also reaches out, affecting those around you. Your fragrance is a testimony of God's favor upon your life. This anointing is the power of God that sets us apart.

> *You love righteousness, and hate wickedness: therefore God, Your God, has **anointed** You with the oil of gladness above Your fellows.*   (Psalm 45:7)

The Hebrew word used here for *"anointing"* is *mashach*, which means "to rub in." When this level of anointing is rubbed into you, your flesh becomes uncomfortable. You might say that it "rubs your flesh the wrong way." Don't panic. You need this to happen because where you're going, your flesh can't take you. That flesh must die in order for your spirit to fly.

In the Spirit, these realms build upon each other. When faith and anointing work together, they destroy the yoke of bondage that faith alone cannot break. When this anointing works within us, it deals with our moral character, producing a greater manifestation of the fruit of the Spirit: *"But the fruit of the Spirit is love, joy, peace, long-suffering, gentleness, goodness, faith, meekness, temperance: against such there is no law"* (Galatians 5:22–23).

Somebody has said, "The anointing is God's gift to mankind, but integrity is mankind's gift back to God." This is true, but the anointing that allows us to walk in full integrity is only discovered when we submit ourselves completely to the work of God's Spirit. We must become marinated by the anointing, allowing it to be rubbed into every area of our life—spirit, soul, and body.

If we receive the things of the Spirit deeply, an infilling brings tenderness to our soul. This doesn't always happen during the initial outpouring of anointing, but as we spend time in God's presence, the anointing increases. We move from the initial outpouring into the covering, and finally into being marinated with an anointing that supernaturally infiltrates the very core of our being. You can't get to the place in the glory that God wants to take you unless you push through in the anointing that He's given you.

Some people want to skip this process, but you can't afford to do that. You must let the anointing work within you. The anointing comes to do a job, and one of its assignments is marinating you in God's process of preparation.

DAY 22

THEY WERE HEALED, EVERY ONE

F. F. BOSWORTH

There came also a multitude out of the cities round about to
Jerusalem, bringing sick folks, and them which were vexed
with unclean spirits: and they were healed every one.
—Acts 5:16

The early church took Christ at His word and prayed unitedly for signs and wonders of healing, until *"the place was shaken where they were assembled together"* (Acts 4:31); and then…

> …*they brought forth the sick into the streets, and laid them on*
> *beds and couches…. There came also a multitude out of the*
> *cities round about to Jerusalem, bringing sick folks, and them*
> *which were vexed with unclean spirits: and they were healed*
> *every one.*   (Acts 5:15–16)

The Gospels describe *"all that Jesus beg+an both to do and teach"* (Acts 1:1). In this incident in the book of Acts, Jesus was continuing His ministry from the right hand of God through His *"body, the church*" (Colossians 1:18), according to His promise. Some say, "Oh, that was only in the beginning of the Acts of the Apostles, for the purpose of confirming their word regarding Christ's resurrection."

Let us, then, turn to the *last* chapter of Acts, and read how, thirty years later, after Paul, on the island of Melita, had healed the father of Publius: "*When this was done, others also, which had diseases in the island, came, and were healed*" (Acts 28:9).

So we see again, even at this time, in the very last chapter of the Acts of the Holy Spirit, which is the only unfinished book of the New Testament, it was still the will of God to heal not some, but *all*.

The Holy Spirit, whom Christ sent as His Successor and Executive, took possession of the church, which is the body of Christ, and showed the same healing power after Pentecost that Christ had displayed before, and vast multitudes were healed. In Acts, as well as the Gospels, we never read of anyone asking for healing and being denied. Men have named this book "The Acts of the Apostles." A better and a truer name for this book would be "The Acts of the Holy Spirit," because it records the acts of the Holy Spirit through not only the apostles, but also other believers. Philip and Stephen, who were not apostles, were as gloriously used as Peter and John. The Holy Spirit came to execute for us all the blessings purchased by Christ's redemption, and pledged by the seven redemptive names. He has never lost any of His interest in the work He came to do. If you wish to know how He wants to act today, read how He has acted. The book of Acts shows us how He wants to act throughout "*always* ["all the days" in Greek], *even to the end of the world* [age]" (Matthew 28:20).

It was the Holy Spirit who worked all the miracles of healing at the hands of Christ. Jesus never undertook a miracle until, in answer to His prayer, the Holy Spirit, the Miracle Worker, came upon Him; and then, in full reliance upon the Spirit, He cast out demons and healed the sick. The miracles of Christ were all done by the Spirit in advance of the Spirit's own dispensation, or before He had yet entered officially into office. Why would the Holy Spirit, who healed all the sick before His dispensation began, do less after He entered office? Did the Miracle Worker enter office to do away with miracles during His own dispensation?

Is the teaching and the practice of the church in the matter of healing in this Laodicean (lukewarm; see Revelation 3:14–18) period of her history a truer expression of the will of God than the teaching and practice of the early church while under the full sway of the Spirit? Decidedly not! I do not hesitate to say that modern theology has robbed the Holy Spirit of a part of His ministry.

DAY 23

THE CHARISMATIC RENEWAL

LESTER SUMRALL

Repent, and be baptized every one of you in the name of
Jesus Christ for the remission of sins, and you shall receive
the gift of the Holy Ghost. For the promise is to you,
and to your children, and to all that are afar off,
even as many as the Lord our God shall call.
—Acts 2:38–39

The charismatic renewal is said to be the fastest growing religious movement since New Testament days, having grown quickly and in many directions. People from every Christian denominational background are coming together, equally eager to receive truth about the charismatic gifts of the Holy Spirit.

During the first half of the twentieth century, the most despised segment of the Christian church was known as "Pentecostalism." Suddenly these Pentecostals have become the most important spiritual factor on the face of the earth.

In the decade of the 1960s, multitudes within the socalled traditional churches—Catholics, Episcopalians, Lutherans,

Methodists, Baptists, and others—started receiving the infilling of the Holy Spirit, just as was experienced by the early disciples on the day of Pentecost, evidenced by a phenomenon called "speaking in other tongues." (See Acts 2:1–4.)

"Tongues" is a spiritual language coming from the spiritual person—not from the "soulical" parts (the mind), but from the spirit. The words spoken cannot be understood by the mind. In this experience, God gives the speaker what is termed a "heavenly language," or a "prayer language."

It was a remarkable and amazing event to the Protestant world when Catholics began to move in spiritual realities, bypassing the entire fundamental and orthodox denominations and entering into the ranks of the Pentecostals—those who believed the whole Bible to be the Full Gospel. When the Spirit began to move them into the salvation rank of regeneration, they went on into the fullness of the baptism of the Holy Spirit. To me it is remarkable that they did not stop halfway. They did not stop on second base, but they ran on around. If they were going to have anything, they would have it all— and they received, much to the amazement of millions of people!

Multitudes of people in this charismatic renewal meet in colleges, in private homes, in borrowed halls. They meet in the most unlikely and unusual places to worship their God and His beloved Son, the Lord Jesus Christ. The gifts of the Spirit function wherever they meet—whether it is in a church, a home, an office building, an auditorium, or a convention hall.

These manifestations clearly demonstrate that God has no "holy" places. He will meet you anywhere—the home, the factory, the street—wherever you are.

Many people teach that after the day of Pentecost, the phenomena of "charisma" ceased. For people to say that God cannot do today what He was doing 2,000 years ago shows me they do not know the God I know. My God can do anything today that He did then. We are not eating the leftovers of a feast; we are taking in the whole menu. We are getting in on the best and the biggest that the world has ever known.

Proof of this is in Acts, chapter 2. On the day of Pentecost, Peter stood and spontaneously began to preach. Under the anointing of the Holy Spirit, he laid open the Word of God and preached with such strength and power that the people trembled at his words. Verse 37 says this of the people who heard:

> Now when they heard this, they were pricked in their heart, and said to Peter and to the rest of the apostles, Men and brethren, what shall we do?

Peter's response was simple:

> Then Peter said to them, Repent, and be baptized every one of you in the name of Jesus Christ for the remission of sins, and you shall receive the gift of the Holy Ghost. For the promise is to you, and to your children, and to all that are afar off, even as many as the Lord our God shall call.   (verses 38–39)

Who is this promise for?

When Peter was speaking to these people, he said, "For the promise is to you, and to your children." The promise had already passed beyond the apostles to those people there before him, then on to their children. But that is not all Peter said. He continued with these important words: "and to all that are afar off, even as many as the Lord our God shall call." That's you and me!

On the day of Pentecost we had the direct promise that what God did at that moment He would never cease to do. The promise was for them, for their children, for all those afar off, even as many as God would call. Since the call of God is the call to repentance, as long as God is saving people, He will also be filling them with His precious Holy Spirit.

DAY 24

HOW THE HOLY SPIRIT MOVES

JAMES W. GOLL

*The earth was without form, and void; and darkness was
upon the face of the deep. And the Spirit of God moved
["was hovering"* ESV] *upon the face of the waters.*
—Genesis 1:2

The Holy Spirit loves messes. How do I know? At creation, as
the Holy Spirit was lingering over the formless nothingness, God
spoke into being the world as we know it. The Spirit of God "loved"
the chaos to life, transforming it from mess to magnificence.

Many Bible scholars apply "the law of first mention" to their
study and interpretation of the Scripture; this principle main-
tains that the first time a word, a concept, or a doctrine is found in
Scripture fixes its characteristics from that point forward. In the
verse above, which is the second verse of the entire Bible, we see
that the Spirit of God *moves.* And that is how He operates to this
day. All the time, He keeps moving across the surface of the earth,
and He brings light into darkness wherever He goes. He didn't

stop moving that way after the earth was created, because He is constantly renewing the face of the earth, along with the hearts of the earth's inhabitants.

The most basic answer to the question "How does the Holy Spirit move?" is that He *hovers*. He stays over something until He chooses to move on, having completed His inspection or implementation. How should we respond to this information? Sometimes, our lives may feel like "formless nothingness," too, but the Holy Spirit within us is not inert. We can respond to His movements within us and around us today. We can open our hearts to receive the grace of God and to release it to others!

How does opening ourselves to the Holy Spirit work in real life? How can we prepare and position our spirits so that we can move with God's Spirit?

Initially, we must learn the value of quieting ourselves. We need to stop hurrying so much. When our spirits and minds are like stirred-up fishbowls or shaken-up snow globes, we can't hear what He's saying. The psalmist knew this secret: "*I wait for the LORD, my soul does wait, and in His word do I hope. My soul waits for the Lord more than they that watch for the morning: I say, more than they that watch for the morning*" (Psalm 130:5–6).

These days, we sometimes call the process of waiting in the presence of the Lord "soaking." This is when you get your spirit's tank refilled with the Holy Spirit, and it is best to establish a pattern of doing it the first thing in the morning so that you can return to that inner place of peace and trust anytime throughout the day, finding your satisfaction in Him. The psalmist compared a quieted soul to a contented young child who has been well cared for, whose hunger has been fully satisfied: "*My soul is even as a weaned child*" (Psalm 131:2).

Once we have quieted ourselves, we can seek out God. Throughout the day, we can exercise the gift of tongues; we can pray in the Spirit. This builds our faith very effectively and turns us toward the Father's heart. Paul wrote to the Corinthians, *"I speak with tongues more than you all"* (1 Corinthians 14:18), and what he meant was that he relied heavily on this gift, to the point that he may have used it more than all of the Corinthians put together.

An important part of opening ourselves to the Holy Spirit is making a conscious determination to be a participant in whatever He wants to do, instead of remaining merely a passive observer. When you go to worship meetings, you should be ready to get involved, eager to give and not only to receive. At the minimum, you should be an intercessor, praying for those who are leading the meeting, "holding up their arms" as Aaron and Hur held up Moses's arms in order to bring victory to the Israelites. (See Exodus 17:8–13.) Stir up your faith and believe that God wants to use "little ole me," as Randy Clark says, to impart His love to others.

Even if you are having a proverbial "bad day," you can still allow God to use you. On your worst day, you've got something alive within you that you can give away. It is the hope of glory. True hope is something the world just does not have. When you are walking and moving in the strength and counsel that the Spirit supplies, you are operating in God's grace.

Ask the Holy Spirit for a fresh revelation of His grace. You already know that you cannot earn the gifts of the Spirit or access the power of God without grace. When you move with the Spirit in God's grace, all the credit and all the glory returns to God, where it belongs.

DAY 25

THE TWOFOLD BLESSING

ANDREW MURRAY

A new heart also will I give you, and a new Spirit will I put within you.... And I will put My Spirit within you.
—Ezekiel 36:26–27

God has revealed Himself in two great covenants. In the old covenant, we have the promise and preparation; in the new covenant, we have fulfillment and possession. In both there is a twofold working of God's Spirit.

In the Old Testament, we have the Spirit of God coming upon men and working on them in special times and ways. In the New Testament, we have the Holy Spirit entering men and women, dwelling within them, and working from within them. In the former, we have the Spirit of God as the Almighty and Holy One. In the latter, we have the Spirit of the Father of Jesus Christ.

We must not think that with the closing of the Old Testament there was no more work of preparation in the New Testament. Just as there were blessed anticipations of the indwelling of God's

Spirit in the Old Testament, the twofold working still continues in the New Testament. Because of a lack of knowledge and faith, a believer may even in these days receive little more than the Old Testament measure of the Spirit's working.

The indwelling Spirit has indeed been given to every child of God. Yet you may experience little beyond the first half of the promise (the new spirit given to us in regeneration) and know almost nothing of God's own Spirit. The Spirit's work in the convicting of sin, and His leading to repentance and the new life, serve as the preparatory work. The distinctive glory of the gift of the Spirit is His divine personal indwelling in the heart of the believer to reveal the Father and the Son. If Christians understand and remember this, they will be able to claim the full blessing prepared for them in Christ Jesus.

In the words of Ezekiel, we find this twofold blessing of God's Spirit presented very strikingly. "*A new Spirit will I put within you*"; that is, man's own spirit is to be renewed and quickened by the work of God's Spirit. When this has been done, there is a second blessing, "*I will put My Spirit within you*"—to dwell in that new spirit. Where God is to dwell, He must have a habitation. With Adam, He had to create a body before He could breathe the spirit of life into him. In Israel, the tabernacle and the temple had to be built and completed before God could come down and take possession. So a new heart is given to us, and a new spirit put within us, as the prerequisite of God's own Spirit being given to dwell within us.

David prayed in Psalm 51, "*Create in me a clean heart, O God; and **renew a right spirit** within me*" (verse 10). He then said, "*Take not **Your holy spirit** from me*" (verse 11). Jesus said, "*That which is born of the **Spirit** is **spirit***" (John 3:6). This indicates that the divine Spirit begets the new spirit in man. The two are distinguished in Romans 8:16: "*The Spirit* [God's Spirit] *itself bears witness **with our spirit**, that we are the children of God.*" Our spirit is the renewed, born-again spirit. Dwelling in us is God's Holy Spirit, yet He is to be distinguished from our spirit, witnessing in and through it.

This distinction helps us to understand the true relationship between rebirth and the indwelling of the Spirit. The new birth is when the Holy Spirit, by convicting us of sin, leads us to repentance and faith in Christ and imparts a new nature. Through the Holy Spirit, God fulfills the promise, "*A new Spirit will I put within you.*" The believer is now a child of God, a temple ready for the Spirit to dwell in.

The second half of the promise is fulfilled as surely as the first when claimed by faith. As long as the believer looks only at rebirth and the renewal of his spirit, he will not come to the life of joy and strength that is meant for him. He must accept God's promise that there is something better than even the new nature.

When he realizes that the Spirit of the Father and the Son can dwell within him, the wonderful prospect of a life of holiness and blessedness is recognized. To fully know this Holy Spirit becomes his one great desire. The believer wants to know how the Spirit works and how he can experience His indwelling and be brought closer to Christ.

DAY 26

DOES GOD ALWAYS HEAL?

JOHN G. LAKE

And these signs shall follow them that believe; in My name…
they shall lay hands on the sick, and they shall recover.
—Mark 16:17–18

In the spiritual world, the spirit of man is the dynamo. It is set in motion by prayer, the desire of the heart. Prayer is a veritable Holy Spirit-controlling dynamo, attracting to itself the Spirit of God. The Spirit of God being received into the spirit of man through prayer is distributed by the action of the will wherever desired. The Spirit of God flowed through the hands of Jesus to the ones who were sick and healed them. It flowed from His soul, wirelessly, to the suffering ones and healed them also.

The will of God to *save* a man is undisputed by intelligent Christians. The will of God to *heal* every man is equally God's purpose. God has not only made provision that, through the Spirit of God received into our lives, our souls may be blessed and our bodies healed, but further we in turn are expected and commanded by Jesus to distribute the Spirit's power to others, that they likewise may be blessed and healed. *"And these signs shall follow them that believe; in My name,"* said Jesus, *"...they shall lay hands on the sick, and they shall recover"* (Mark 16:17–18). This refers not to a special priest or a particular individual endowed with peculiar powers, but to the *believer,* the everyday man who accepts the gospel of Jesus Christ and who becomes a declared disciple of the Son of God. (See Mark 16:14–20.)

On the Day of Pentecost, when the floodtide of the Holy Spirit broke over the church at Jerusalem and its glory-power radiated through their souls and rested upon them as tongues of fire and they were filled with the Holy Ghost and began to speak with other tongues as the *Spirit* gave them utterance, the people demanded an explanation of the phenomena. (See Acts 2:1–12.)

Peter replied,

This Jesus has God raised up [resurrection], *whereof we all are witnesses. Therefore being by the right hand of God exalted* [ascension], *and having received of the Father the promise of the Holy Ghost* [fulfillment of the promise of the Father], *He has shed forth this, which you now see and hear.*

(Acts 2:32–33)

Through His crucifixion and through His victory over the grave, Jesus secured from the Father the privilege of shedding the Holy Spirit abroad over the world. This was the crowning climax of the redemptive power of God ministered through Jesus Christ to the world. And from that day to this, every soul is entitled to embrace to himself this blessed Spirit of God, which Jesus regarded so valuable to mankind, so necessary for their healing and salvation, that He gave His life to obtain it.

Consequently, it is not a question, "Does God always heal?" That is childish. It is rather a question, "Are we willing to embrace His healing?" If so, it is for us to receive. More than this, it is for all the world to receive, for every man to receive who will put his nature in contact with God through opening his heart to the Lord.

Jesus, knowing the world's need of healing, provided definitely for physicians (disciples, ministers, priests, healers) who would minister, not pills and potions, but the *power of God*. The gift of healing is one of the nine gifts of the Spirit provided for and perpetuated forever in the church. (See 1 Corinthians 12:8–11.)

It is an evidence of ignorance of God's Word to continue to discuss the question, "Does God always heal?" as though God healed sometimes, and sometimes He did not. Enlightenment by the Spirit of God, through the Word, reveals that God always was the Healer, is the Healer today, will be the Healer forever. The Word says, *"Jesus Christ the same yesterday, and to day, and for ever"* (Hebrews 13:8). Consequently, there is healing from every disease for every man who will, in faith, embrace the Spirit of God promised by the Father and ministered through Jesus Christ to the souls and bodies of all who desire the blessing.

Peter, in his exposition of this fact said, *"By whose stripes you were healed"* (1 Peter 2:24). The use of *"were"* in this text indicates that the healing was accomplished in the mind of God when Jesus Christ gave Himself as the eternal sacrifice and has never had to be done over again for the healing of any individual. He *willed* it once; it is done forever. He made the provision and invites the world to embrace it. It is yours to have, yours to enjoy, and yours to impart to others.

DAY 27

POWER TO HEAL

FRANCES HUNTER

And by the hands of the apostles were many signs and won-
ders wrought among the people; (and they were all with one
accord in Solomon's porch.... And believers were the more
added to the Lord, multitudes both of men and women.)
Insomuch that they brought forth the sick into the streets, and
laid them on beds and couches, that at the least the shadow of
Peter passing by might overshadow some of them.
—Acts 5:12, 14–15

I get so excited because I know that the power of God has not lessened one iota! His power never changes. *"Jesus Christ is the same yesterday, today, and forever"* (Hebrews 13:7–8 NKJV).

The Word of God is anointed and powerful today as I read it and write it down. My office and home are both filled with the power and the presence of God. With every ounce of belief and every ounce of faith that I have in me, I believe that if you will take this Word of God like a medicine, it will work for you. Don't just take it once and stop. As I am instructing you by the Spirit of God, take His Word over and over again into your very spirit, into your very being, into the innermost part of your heart. I believe His Word will heal you of whatever your disease may be.

Jesus gave to the disciples the power to heal all manner of disease. He has not taken that power away from people in this day and age. Right now, let us be in one accord! The early Christians had so much faith, and they were all in one accord. They brought people and laid them on the streets so that even the shadow, just the shadow, of Peter passing by might touch some of them, and they would be healed.

> *There came also a multitude out of the cities round about to Jerusalem, bringing sick folks, and them which were vexed with unclean spirits: and they were healed every one.*
>
> (Acts 5:16)

God has not changed. God has promised us that someday, Charles and I will walk into an auditorium and wave our hands, and every person in that auditorium will be totally and completely healed by the power of God. This will not be because of us but because of the power of God and the working of His Holy Spirit.

Jesus has gone to heaven, but He still lives on earth through us as believers. We are acting in the power of the same Holy Spirit as the first disciples did.

> *Therefore they that were scattered abroad went every where preaching the word. Then Philip went down to the city of Samaria, and preached Christ to them. And the people with one accord gave heed to those things which Philip spoke, hearing and seeing the miracles which he did. For unclean spirits, crying with loud voice, came out of many that were possessed with them: and many taken with palsies, and that were lame, were healed. And there was great joy in that city.* (Acts 8:4–8)

There is no faster way to make people come to Jesus than to let them see miracles.

Philip spoke, and look what happened. The unclean spirits cried and came out. There were many who were possessed; there were many who had palsy; there were many who were lame, and they were healed. Why? Because of the power of God.

There is bound to be great joy in any city when everybody gets healed. I can't wait for that day. I think that will be one of the most exciting days of my entire life. God will probably hold it off until just before the rapture, because He knows I probably wouldn't be able to stand it if it happened before. Hallelujah!

Pray this prayer:

Father, I want You to work through me every day. Jesus, live in me and use me whenever and wherever someone is hurting and in need of Your healing power! Holy Spirit, give me the wisdom and understanding necessary to be used every day of my life. In Jesus's name. Amen.

DAY 28

AVAILABLE TO ALL BELIEVERS

JOAN HUNTER

*When He, the Spirit of truth, is come, He will guide you into
all truth: for He shall not speak of Himself; but whatsoever
He shall hear, that shall He speak: and He will show you
things to come. He shall glorify Me: for He shall receive of
Mine, and shall show it to you.*
—John 16:13–14

At the conclusion of every meeting my parents held, my father,
Charles Hunter, would minister salvation, followed by the baptism in the Holy Spirit. He would then ask for a volunteer from
among the group of newly saved and baptized individuals. Guided
by my father's words, the volunteer would lay hands on someone
who needed a healing miracle, and it would manifest. Night after
night, this process was a powerful demonstration of the truth
that "if Charles and Frances Hunter can do it, you can do it, too!"
Even young children experienced the joy of allowing God's healing
power to flow through their small hands to adults, resulting in the
manifestation of a miraculous healing right before their eyes.

Experienced or inexperienced, old or young, male or female, all of God's children can be empowered to minister healing to one another, as well as to themselves. Why don't more people know about this important aspect of ministry? Because they haven't experienced firsthand the power of God to heal.

For many, many years, the church did not teach that healing and miracles were available to believers. The idea of God's power to heal became strange and mysterious. Even the baptism in the Holy Spirit was considered something that only happened in the early years of the church. The supernatural was avoided by mainstream Christians rather than embraced as an everyday reality for the average believer. Christian leaders deliberately ignored this entire facet of Jesus's ministry, and anyone who believed that God's miraculous blessings are available for the modern-day believer was laughed at and ostracized at times.

Thank goodness some hung on to their beliefs and boldly proclaimed the truth throughout the ages! The Bible is not vague in its teachings on the supernatural, including miraculous healings. You cannot afford to be embarrassed about or selective in your beliefs—nor would you want to! From cover to cover, the Bible is Truth. Ask God to open your eyes to His Truth—the real Truth, in its entirety. If you have God's Holy Spirit living within you, greater understanding of the Scriptures is not only possible; it is promised. (See John 16:7, 13–14.)

Again, the Christian life must not be confined to mere study of the Bible, resulting in knowledge without application. True Christianity is a wonderful journey—an ongoing experience of the supernatural power of God living and working through you. Daily dependence on God is a necessary element. You will not be trapped in theology and/or a lifestyle void of the supernatural in which you need God only occasionally. You will not avoid places where supernatural healing manifests. Instead, you will actively search for the exciting moves of God and jump into the flow of

God's true purpose for your life. You will participate, not just observe.

What is religion keeping you from doing? Don't let it rob you of a deep, meaningful relationship with your heavenly Father, Jesus, and His Holy Spirit.

Returning home one day, I talked to a neighbor and said, "I just got back from a miracle service, and it was great!"

"Oh," she replied, "all those people that fall on the floor are actually demon-possessed."

Nothing could be further from the truth! Someone who confuses a miraculous manifestation for demonic possession has never experienced or witnessed the supernatural. When you are slain in the Spirit, you become so full of the Holy Spirit that you can't even stand. You pass out at the overwhelming greatness of God's presence when He overshadows you and short-circuits your central nervous system. You suddenly find yourself lying peacefully on the floor while God's healing power flows through you.

If you don't have the necessary knowledge to understand this type of experience, you will view it through natural eyes and interpret it with man's limited understanding, and you will never be prepared to receive all the blessings that God has planned for you.

At one time, my children said, "You know, Mom, you should just quit the ministry. You are under such great attack. Just quit."

I will be the first to admit, I have been knocked down a few times. I have run over a few potholes along the way. However, whenever this happens, I just get back up, dust myself off, and keep on going. That is what you are supposed to do also. The devil may try to hinder me, and man may trip me up, but I just get up and keep on going. These areas of attack were brought on by others' decisions, not God!

Pray with me:

Father, open my eyes to Your Truth. Allow me to see and experience Your Holy Spirit working through me as I pray for healing miracles for others as well as myself. Help me embrace Your supernatural workings in my life. You always do things for my good, my provision, and my protection. Thank You for Your love. In Jesus's name. Amen.

DAY 29

THE SPIRIT COMES IN MANY WAYS

MARIA WOODWORTH-ETTER

I will pour out of My Spirit upon all flesh:
and your sons and your daughters shall prophesy, and your
young men shall see visions, and your old men shall dream
dreams: and on My servants and on My handmaidens I will
pour out in those days of My Spirit.
—Acts 2:17–18

God will not only come in healing power, but will manifest Himself in many mighty ways. On the Day of Pentecost, *Peter said,* "[*Jesus*] *has shed forth this, which you now see and hear*" (*Acts 2:33*). *And from what they saw and heard, three thousand acknowledged that it was the power of God and turned to Christ. Others stifled conviction and turned away, saying, "This is the work of the devil." When the Holy Spirit is poured out, it is either "life to life" or "death to death"* (2 Corinthians 2:16). It is "*life to life*" to those who go forward and "*death to death*" to those who blaspheme against the Holy Spirit. So we want to be careful what we say against the diverse operations, supernatural signs, and workings of the Holy Spirit. Some people look on and say,

"It looks like hypnotism" or "I believe they are mesmerized." To others, it appears to be mere foolishness, even as the Scripture says of the "natural man": "the things of the Spirit of God:…are foolishness to him…because they are spiritually discerned" (1 Corinthians 2:14).

It was the same on the day of Pentecost, when a multitude saw the disciples staggering about under the power of the Spirit, speaking in tongues. While some said, "They are drunk" (see Acts 2:13), others knew that the mighty power of God was there.

There is a power here that is not of earth, a power lifting people up, making men and women upright, making them good neighbors, good husbands and wives. It is the mighty presence of Almighty God. Observe the lives of these people. They do not seek worldly amusements, but the power of God is manifested in them.

What did the power bring on the day of Pentecost? The people who came together were all amazed and said, "We never saw anything like this before." Everybody became convicted, though some, who were not willing to accept it, not willing to be called fools for Christ's sake, rejected it. To ease their guilty consciences, they said, "They are drunk."

They knew better. They knew that the mighty power of God was there; if there was a question about it, God settled it. Peter got up in the midst of them and said, "These are not drunken, as you suppose, seeing it is but the third hour of the day. But this is that which was spoken by the prophet Joel; and it shall come to pass in the last days, says God, I will pour out of My Spirit upon all flesh: and your sons and your daughters shall prophesy, and your young men shall see visions, and your old men shall dream dreams: and on My servants and on My handmaidens I will pour out in those days of My Spirit" (Acts 2:15–18).

It is the same Holy Spirit today. The Holy Spirit is the Spirit of God. He is a person, and He works under the direction of Jesus Christ, under His orders. He doesn't do anything except what Christ tells Him to do. When we are ready to receive Him, Jesus sends the Holy Spirit to impart to us His own gifts. The Holy Spirit cleanses these temples of ours and comes in to dwell. He fills our bodies, and His power in us gives us utterances in tongues (see Acts 2:4) and works through us in other ways.

I love the Holy Spirit because He is always witnessing for Jesus, and He comes to bring us power. (See Acts 1:8.) He is *"the Comforter...the Spirit of truth"* (John 15:26) who will abide forever. (See John 14:16.) He brings all things to our remembrances (see John 14:26). We are so forgetful in our natural state. But we have spiritual minds, and God writes His Word on our minds and on the tablets of our hearts. (See Hebrews 10:16.) The Holy Spirit brings these messages to us at the right time—a message to this one who is in sin, that one who is in sorrow—messages from heaven that encourage the weak and help the strong and always point us to Jesus, the great Burden-Bearer.

DAY 30

GOD'S SUPERMAN

E. W. KENYON

With God all things are possible.
—Matthew 19:26

Jesus uttered some prophetic facts about believers.

Jesus is uttering a fact, and here is its compliment: *"Nothing shall be impossible to you"* (Matthew 17:20).

Take this with Mark 11:24: *"What things soever you desire, when you pray, believe that you receive them, and you shall have them."*

Or take Mark 9:23: *"All things are possible to him that believes."*

The word *"believes"* means "a believing one." There were no "believing ones" in the time while Christ was preaching. They were Jews under law. The "believing ones" came into being at Pentecost. It meant a believer, a "new creation man."

The new creation man is a partaker of God's nature. He is really an Incarnation. He has received the nature and life of God. Then he invites the Spirit who raised Jesus from the dead, who came on the day of Pentecost, to make His home in his body. This man not only has God's nature, but has God actually living in him.

If this doesn't constitute a superman, then I don't know what a superman is.

But I am going to carry you one step farther.

This man, with God dwelling in him, is given a legal right to the use of the name of Jesus with the power of attorney. The question is: What is that name worth? What authority is there behind it?

Matthew 28:18–20 Jesus says, *"All power is given to Me in heaven and in earth. Go you therefore* [with this authority]*, and teach all nations…teaching them to observe all things whatsoever I have commanded you: and, lo, I am with you always, even to the end of the world."*

You see what we have now? We have the power of attorney to use the name of Jesus; and all authority in heaven and on earth is invested in that name.

Go over it just once more.

The believer is a new creation. The old things of weakness and failure have passed away and behold the old man has become a new man and all these things are of God. (See 2 Corinthians 5:17.)

This man is a partaker of the divine nature, eternal life: *"He that has the Son has life"* (1 John 5:12).

Now he has the Holy Spirit indwelling him: *"Greater is He that is in you, than he that is in the world"* (1 John 4:4).

This believer, this new creation, is a child of Deity. He stands before the world as a very branch of the vine. He is taking Jesus's place in the world.

And if this isn't a superman, then I don't know the meaning of the term.

The church has kept this "Samson" imprisoned by false teachings and by creeds and doctrines. They have not only held him a prisoner to their philosophies and dogmas, but they have actually put out his eyes.

But the Father is going to restore sight to him and break the bonds that hold him.

DAY 31

HOW TO RECEIVE AN OUTPOURING OF THE HOLY SPIRIT

GUILLERMO MALDONADO

*And it shall come to pass afterward, that I will pour out My
Spirit upon all flesh; and your sons and your daughters shall
prophesy, your old men shall dream dreams,
your young men shall see visions.*
—Joel 2:28

Amid the problems, difficulties, and great amount of misinformation we receive every day, we often fail to look for what really matters in our lives. The outpouring of the Holy Spirit should be a priority for us. From there, every problem, impossibility, or crisis will come under the control of the Spirit and will be solved by the power of God. How do we receive that outpouring? Let's look at some contexts that lead to this outpouring.

Many people come to have an encounter with the supernatural when they have no other choice—when they are suffering from a terminal illness, a family problem, or a seemingly-impossible situation that leaves them perplexed and not knowing what to do. It is then that they realize only God can change their reality.

> As the deer pants for the water brooks, so pants my soul for You, O God. My soul thirsts for God, for the living God. When shall I come and appear before God?
>
> (Psalm 42:1–2 NKJV)

When we are tired of the attacks of the devil and of situations that defeat us, when people are not changing or turning away from their rebellion against God, then we enter a desperation for a divine intervention, for an outpouring of His Spirit.

Are you only satisfied with what God has done in the past? Are you content just reading miracle stories in the Bible—or do you want to be a part of those miracles? Are you satisfied with traditional Christianity—or are you desperate for a change? Do you know deep inside that there is more to life than what you have experienced and that we are in the middle of a spiritual awakening? Do you want a revival in your life? Do you want an awakening in your family and in your city? Are you willing to pay the price to be used by God in miracles, signs, and wonders? If you are desperate for a change or a revival, the Spirit is willing to pour Himself out upon you, your family, your ministry, and your city.

The anointing and the power of the Holy Spirit are two of the ways God works through a person, and both operate by the "law of exchange." "For He whom God has sent speaks the words of God: for God gives not the Spirit by measure" (John 3:34). God gives us anointing and power without measure, but how much we receive depends on the priority we give to that impartation. The more we surrender to the Holy Spirit, the more we will have of Him. That is why Paul said, "I am crucified with Christ: nevertheless I live; yet not I, but Christ lives in me: and the life which I now live in the flesh I live by the faith of the Son of God, who loved me, and gave Himself for me" (Galatians 2:20).

The measure of the Holy Spirit and power that you have are a mark of how much of yourself you have surrendered to God. If you have only given 50 percent, that is the space available in your spirit, and the limit of anointing and power you can receive. Another way of saying this is that you harvest in proportion to what you sow; no more and no less. If you give yourself completely to the Holy Spirit, He will give Himself entirely to you.

We all have areas to surrender to God: our rights, natural fears, insecurities, jealousy, and, of course, the flesh. We must let go of wicked thoughts, anger, unforgiveness, stubbornness, old scars, sexual immorality. We must let it all go to make room for more of the Spirit.

You must make the decision to give more of yourself and ask for more from Him; to want more of Him and less of you. Jesus was so hungry for the Father's will that He died to Himself to such a degree that the Father gave Him both the anointing and the spirit of power without measure.

When Jesus said, *"Most assuredly, I say to you, he who believes in Me, the works that I do he will do also; and greater works than these he will do, because I go to My Father"* (John 14:12 NKJV), He was talking about the mark that should distinguish every believer.

We can all carry and release an outpouring. The Holy Spirit is one and the same for all. That means that every believer has the same potential as Peter, Paul, or the best preacher of our century. We all have the same capacity to be used by God. Regardless of your gender, nationality, race, or social status, you can be used by the Holy Spirit now.

DAY 32

THE HOLY SPIRIT—THE SPIRIT OF HEALING

ANDREW MURRAY

Now there are diversities of gifts, but the same Spirit....
To another faith by the same Spirit; to another the gifts of
healing by the same Spirit;...but all these works that one and
the selfsame Spirit, dividing to every man severally as He will.
—1 Corinthians 12:4, 9, 11

The gift of healing is one of the most beautiful manifestations of the Spirit. It is recorded of Jesus, *"God anointed Jesus of Nazareth with the Holy Ghost and with power: who went about doing good, and healing all that were oppressed of the devil"* (Acts 10:38). The Holy Spirit in Him was a healing Spirit, and He was the same in the disciples after Pentecost. Thus, the words of our text express what was the continuous experience of the early churches. (See Acts 3:7; 4:30; 5:12, 15–16; 6:8; 8:7; 9:41; 14:9–10; 16:18–19; 19:12; 28:8–9.) The abundant outpouring of the Spirit produced abundant healings. What a lesson for the church in our day!

Divine healing is the work of the Holy Spirit. Christ's redemption extends its powerful working to the body, and the Holy Spirit is in charge of transmitting it to us and maintaining it in us, Our bodies share in the benefit of the redemption, and even now we can receive the pledge of it by divine healing. It is Jesus who heals, Jesus who anoints and baptizes with the Holy Spirit, and Jesus who baptized His disciples with the same Spirit. It is He who sends us the Holy Spirit here on earth to take sickness away from us and to restore us to health.

Divine healing accompanies the sanctification by the Spirit. The Holy Spirit makes us partakers of Christ's redemption in order to make us holy. Hence His name "Holy." Therefore, the healing that He works is an intrinsic part of His divine mission. He bestows this healing to lead the sick one to be converted and to believe (see Acts 4:29–30; 5:12, 14; 6:7–8; 8:6, 8; 9:42) or to confirm his faith if he is already converted. The Spirit constrains him thus to renounce sin and to consecrate himself entirely to God and to His service. (See 1 Corinthians 11:31; James 5:15–16; Hebrews 12:10.)

Divine healing glorifies Jesus. It is God's will that His Son should be glorified, and the Holy Spirit does this when He comes to show us what the redemption of Christ does for us. The redemption of the mortal body appears almost more marvelous than that of the immortal soul. In these two ways, God wills to dwell in us through Christ, and thus to triumph over the flesh. As soon as our bodies become the temple of God through the Spirit, Jesus is glorified.

Divine healing takes place wherever the Spirit of God works in power. Examples of this are to be found in the lives of the reformers, and in other men of God called to His service over the centuries. But there are even more promises accompanying the outpouring of the Holy Spirit that have not been fulfilled up to this time. Let us live in a holy expectation, praying for the Lord to accomplish them in us.

DAY 33

THE HOLY SPIRIT'S ROLE IN REVIVAL

CHARLES FINNEY

O Lord, revive Your work.
—Habakkuk 3:2

A revival can be expected when Christians have the spirit of prayer for a revival—that is, when they pray as if their hearts were set on it. Sometimes, Christians do not use a definite prayer for a revival, even when they are inspired in prayer. Their minds are on something else—the salvation of the lost—and they are not praying for a revival among themselves. But when they feel the lack of a revival, they will pray for it. People feel for their own families and neighborhoods, so they will earnestly pray for them.

What constitutes the spirit of prayer? Is it fervent words and many prayers? No. Prayer is the state of the heart. The spirit of prayer is a state of continual desire and anxiety for the salvation of sinners. It can even be something that weighs a person down. It is the same, as far as the philosophy of mind is concerned, as when a person is concerned with some worldly interest. A Christian who has this spirit of prayer feels concerned for souls. They are always on his mind. He thinks of them by day and dreams of them by night. This is "praying without ceasing." (See 1 Thessalonians 5:17.) His prayers seem to flow from his heart like water: "O LORD, *revive Your work*" (Habakkuk 3:2). Sometimes this feeling is very deep.

This is by no means fanaticism. It is just what Paul felt when he said, "*My little children, of whom I travail in birth*" (Galatians 4:19). This labor of soul is that deep agony people feel when they hold on to God for a blessing and will not let Him go until they receive it. I do not mean to say that it is essential to have this great distress in order to have the spirit of prayer. But the deep, continual, earnest desire for the salvation of sinners is what constitutes the spirit of prayer for a revival.

When this desire exists in a church, unless the Spirit is grieved away by sin, there will always be a revival of Christians. Generally, it will involve the conversion of sinners to Jesus. A clergyman once told me of a revival among his people that started with a zealous and devoted woman in the church. She became concerned about sinners and started praying for them. She prayed, and her distress increased. She finally went to her minister and talked with him, asking him to schedule an evangelistic meeting. She felt that one was needed. The minister put her off because he did not feel the same need. The next week she came again, asking him to schedule a meeting. She knew people would come because she felt God was going to pour out His Spirit. The minister put her off once more. Finally, she said to him, "If you do not schedule the meeting, I will die, because there is going to be a revival." The next Sunday, he scheduled a meeting. He said that if anyone wished to talk with him about the salvation of his soul, he would meet with him. He did not know of anyone who was concerned over his soul, but when he went to the appointed place, he was surprised to find a large number of anxious inquirers.

Do you think that woman knew there was going to be a revival? Call it what you like, a new revelation or an old revelation or anything else. It was the Spirit of God who showed that praying woman there was going to be a revival. The secret of the Lord was with her, and she knew it. She knew God had been in her heart and had filled it so full that she could not hold it in.

A revival is near when Christians begin to confess their sins to one another. Usually they confess in a general, halfhearted manner. They may do it in eloquent language, but it means nothing. But when there is an honest breaking down and a pouring out of the heart in confession of sin, the floodgates will soon burst open, and salvation will flow everywhere.

A revival can be expected when Christians are willing to make the sacrifices necessary to carry it on. They must be willing to sacrifice their feelings, business, and time to help the work. Ministers must be willing to expend their energy. They must be willing to offend the impenitent by plain and faithful speech and perhaps offend many members of the church who will not repent. They must take a stand regarding the revival, whatever the consequences. They must be prepared to go on with the work even though they risk losing the affection of the impenitent and cold members of the church. The minister must be prepared, if it is the will of God, to be driven away from the place. He must be determined to go straight forward, leaving the event in God's hands.

DAY 34

THE ANOINTING BREAKS THE YOKE

MARILYN HICKEY

And it shall come to pass in that day, that his burden shall be
taken away from off your shoulder,
and his yoke from off your neck, and the yoke shall be
destroyed because of the anointing.
—Isaiah 10:27

I have noticed that healing always comes by the power of the Holy Spirit:

> *God anointed Jesus of Nazareth with the Holy Spirit and with power, who went about doing good and healing all who were oppressed by the devil, for God was with Him.* (Acts 10:38)

The Father heals because He is merciful and compassionate, and the Son heals because He does what the Father does. However, as I mentioned briefly before, Jesus doesn't heal just by the Father's love and compassion; He heals by the *anointing*. The Word reveals that Jesus didn't heal the sick until after He was anointed with the Holy Spirit. (See, for example, Mark 1:10–12, 23–34.)

Jesus was endued with power from the Spirit of God; that power or anointing was what healed and delivered. Did you know the Father promised the same anointing for those who are born again? Jesus, referring to this anointing as the baptism with the Holy Spirit, commanded that every believer receive it. (See Acts 1:4–5, 8.) That anointing came for the first time on the day of Pentecost. (See Acts 2:1–4.) Peter afterward declared that the same experience is for us, for our children, and *to all that are afar off, even as many as the Lord our God shall call* (Acts 2:39).

The anointing brings healing because it breaks the yoke of Satan's bondage:

> *And it shall come to pass in that day, that his burden shall be taken away from off your shoulder, and his yoke from off your neck, **and the yoke shall be destroyed because of the anointing.*** (Isaiah 10:27)

The apostle Paul was very much aware that it was the anointing that gave him the power to accomplish anything for God. In Romans 15:17–19, he carefully gave the Spirit of God credit for any and all of the mighty signs and wonders that were manifested through him as he preached the gospel.

God always wants to confirm His Word with healing and deliverance, products that serve as evidence of the power and anointing of the Holy Spirit. The Lord yearns for you to receive His anointing; He wants to work miracles through your hands. He has promised believers that they shall lay hands on the sick, and the sick shall recover. Quoting Jesus, Mark wrote,

> *And these signs shall follow them that believe; in My name shall they cast out devils; they shall speak with new tongues; they shall take up serpents; and if they drink any deadly thing,*

> *it shall not hurt them; they shall lay hands on the sick, and*
> *they shall recover.* (Mark 16:17–18)

The anointing of the Holy Spirit does much more than heal bodies, as the above Scriptures attest. It breaks every yoke and enables us to walk not only in health, but also in full vigor. I continually confess that, according to Romans 8:11, the Spirit of Him who raised up Jesus from the dead dwells in me, and He who raised Christ from the dead is quickening, or giving life to, my mortal body by His Spirit who dwells in me. There is nothing quite so valuable as personalizing the promises of God.

Once, at a series of meetings where I was speaking, I really needed the quickening and invigorating power of the Holy Spirit in my body, and I was ever so grateful for that promise. The evangelist who held the meetings is a very vibrant man who enjoys fellowship. After the first evening meeting, which lasted until 11:00 p.m., I intended to refresh my body with a good night's rest since I was the morning speaker. However, a time of food and fellowship was planned for after the service, and I didn't retire until after 2:00 a.m.! A time of fellowship was planned for the ministry people between each of the services, and I thought I was being "revived to a rag," one of my husband's favorite expressions.

I looked around at the rest of the people and thought, *Isn't this getting to them?* But they looked and acted refreshed, and I realized I was being refreshed, as well. The Holy Spirit was quickening my mortal body. Now, I don't recommend that anyone "burn the candle at both ends"; proper rest is part of taking care of the body. However, in the fellowship of the Holy Spirit and in the midst of ministering under the anointing, we had all been refreshed rather than exhausted. The Lord will sustain you physically in all kinds of situations and circumstances when necessary. He will quicken your mortal body.

DAY 35

WORKING MIRACLES IN THE SPIRIT'S ANOINTING

JOSHUA MILLS

*Verily, verily, I say to you, he that believes on Me, the works
that I do shall he do also; and greater works than these shall
he do; because I go to My Father.*
—John 14:12

The dictionary defines the word *miracle* as "an effect or extraordinary event in the physical world that surpasses all known human or natural powers and is ascribed to a supernatural cause." That makes it impossible to do this in the natural. A miracle is something only God can do. The amazing thing is that He wants to release His miracles through you and me.

There are some requirements for being a modern-day miracle worker. The first qualification for operating in creative miracles is that you must have faith for miracles. That coincides with the first realm in the spiritual dimension, the realm of faith. Faith comes by hearing God's Word, and that Word becomes the power of God inside us.

The second qualification for operating in creative miracles is that you must be anointed with power. That coincides with the second realm in the Spirit, the realm of the anointing. It is impossible to work such miracles in our own strength. We need faith to believe that we have been anointed to work miracles in the name of Jesus Christ by the power of the Holy Spirit.

The third qualification for operating successfully in the miraculous is in yielding to God and flowing in His glory. More miracles happen in that realm, and they happen quickly.

The late Frances Hunter, one of my mentors in healing, often said, "Looking for feelings instead of healings can rob you of what God wants to do through you." Remember that God's love is the greatest power available to us. It is available at all times, whether we feel it or not. We cannot be moved by feelings. We must be moved by *fillings*. If we're filled with the Holy Spirit and anointed by Him, then that's enough.

Great miracles happen when we develop compassion for the sick and hurting because God's love flows through us. When we pray out of genuine compassion, we don't pray for them in the natural, out of pity. Compassion means we actually feel their pain and recognize how very much God loves them and wants them to be healed. In sensing what heaven has in store for them, we release God's love upon them. When we operate in God's love, miracles happen. Believe that God wants to do it, and He will.

What does working miracles look like? Faith always takes action. The same faith that saved you brings you healing, but your faith must be confirmed by a specific action. Hebrews 11:6 says, *"Without faith it is impossible to please Him: for he that comes to God must believe that He is, and that He is a rewarder of them that diligently seek Him."* We're not asking God to do anything new or unusual. This is key to understanding the dimension of the miraculous. The atmosphere of miracles is already available to us, just as electricity is always available to us. Instead of asking God to do something, we're simply thanking Him for what He has already done and tapping into what already exists. He is the Rewarder. We just receive His supernatural gift by cooperating with the Spirit.

The way God releases His healing through you varies according to the situation and the specific instruction you receive from heaven. This requires your willingness to flow in obedience with the anointing.

When we launch into miracle ministry, fully trusting God to work through us, we will get "God results." Let the supernatural become your natural. This may sound like an oxymoron, but God wants a flow of miraculous power to become a natural occurrence in our lives.

Since we are all different, what this flow looks like will also be different. Each of us has his or her own method. In whatever way God ministers through you, that's the right way. When you lay hands on the sick, you will have your own style, your own way of praying, your own form of speech, your own vocal inflections, and your own facial expressions. Do what is natural for you. Be natural in being supernatural. Let the power of God flow naturally through you. He created you to operate in this way.

DAY 36

THE CONSCIOUSNESS OF CHRISTIANITY

JOHN G. LAKE

All power is given to Me in heaven and in earth.
—Matthew 28:18

In the soul of Jesus there grew that wonderful consciousness that, having liberated [His disciples] from death's power, there was a step further yet to go. He must take captive the power that was binding their souls. So He entered into death, and His ministry and victory in the regions of death was the result. And one day He came forth from the dead, a living man once more, as He was before He died.

Over and over again, John tells us that He did this and He performed that work and He wrought that marvel in order that we might believe, in order that He might reveal to the satisfaction of the souls of those who were trying to believe that there was a foundation and a reason and a substantial ground on which their confidence in Christ could rest.

So He came forth from the dead with the consciousness of God and His power and His ability to command God's power and utilize it, that no other in all the earth or sea or heaven ever had. No philosopher ever had it, or had ever known anything of it. But when Jesus came forth from the dead, He came forth speaking a word that had never been spoken in the world before. He said, *"All power is given to Me in heaven and in earth."* Blessed be the name of God! He had proven it. Faith had become fact; vision was now consciousness.

All the triumph of Jesus in the regions of death had wrought in His soul the wonder of God. No other life ever had it. No other soul ever got the flame of it. No other nature ever felt the burning of it. Bless God.

And He was so anxious to lift His followers into it that the very first thing He did after His reappearance among them was to *breathe* on them. He said, "Let Me give it to you. Let Me breathe it into your life." *"Receive you the Holy Ghost"* (John 20:22). Let me put it into your hearts, burn it into your soul, establish it into your nature. His victory over death had wrought the marvel.

But, beloved, that is not *Christianity.* Christianity is *more than that.* That is not the consciousness of Christianity. The consciousness of Christianity is greater than that. It was holier than that, more powerful than resurrection consciousness. When Jesus came forth from the dead, He was able to declare, *"All power is given to Me in heaven and in earth. Go you therefore..."* (Matthew 28:18–19).

Oh, then there were some wonderful days—forty wonderful days in which Jesus took the disciples, who had been in His own school for three-and-a-half years, through a new course. In these days, we would call it postgraduate course. So, they went out into the mountains of Galilee, all by themselves, for a postgraduate course with the risen Lord. And He taught them of the power of

God, and He taught them of power over death and the divine fact that the dominion of the risen Christ is for every soul.

So, one day, there came the ascension. He took them out on the Mount of Olives and, as He blessed them, He rose out of their sight to glory. Then, there is one of those wonderful divine flashes in the Word of God that just illuminates a whole life.

Peter was preaching on the day of Pentecost. The power of God had fallen upon the people. The people demanded an explanation. "What is it? What does it mean?" Peter replied, *"This is that which was spoken by the prophet Joel"* (Acts 2:16). Then, he went on and taught them concerning Christ, took them from His crucifixion through His resurrection and His ascension up to the throne of God. And when he got the people at the throne of God and their minds fixed there, he gave them the final explanation: when Jesus had arrived at the throne of God, an interview between God the Father and Jesus Christ took place. And God gave to Jesus the gift of the Holy Ghost, and the explanation was, *"He has shed forth this, which you now see and hear"* (verse 33).

Say, beloved, the Holy Ghost is born out of the heart of the Father God Himself, ministered through the soul of Jesus Christ, the High Priest of God, into your heart and mine. It is intended to lift our hearts and lift our lives out of Chicago mud and to keep us there forever.

So, the real Christian ought to be the kingliest man in the whole earth, the princeliest man in the whole earth—as kingly and princely and lovely and holy as the Son of God—as big as Jesus, with the power of Jesus and the love of Jesus. Bless God.

DAY 37

THE ENEMY'S STRATEGY

MARY K. BAXTER

For we...worship God in the Spirit, and rejoice in Christ Jesus, and have no confidence in the flesh.
—Philippians 3:3

In our own strength, we are helpless to resist the devil's temptations and accusations. God's children are often confused, paralyzed, and even driven to despair when they are exposed to the merciless attacks of the accuser. However, you don't have to be a victim; you can be a victor! Knowledge of the Word will help you to wage spiritual warfare against the devil and the forces of evil in his kingdom.

Since we war against unseen forces, we must wage our battles by faith and not by sight. (See 2 Corinthians 5:7.) We cannot fight back in our own strength; we must remember to rely on the power of the Holy Spirit, and not our own resources, in our battles with the enemy. The apostle Peter learned this lesson the hard way.

Self-confidence prompted him to declare his willingness to die for Christ, but the Lord warned him,

> *Simon, Simon, behold, Satan has desired to have you, that he may sift you as wheat: but I have prayed for you, that your faith fail not: and when you are converted, strengthen your brethren.* (Luke 22:31–32)

Peter's rash boasting in his own abilities to remain faithful to Christ opened the door for the devil to cause him to fall. Jesus told Peter the devil's plan ahead of time and promised to intercede for him. Peter's failures, and the subsequent accusations of the devil, would sift Peter like wheat, confusing him, demoralizing him, and making him vulnerable to losing his faith. But Jesus's prayers sustained him.

Although Peter denied his Lord in fear three times, he repented, and His relationship with Christ was restored. Because of Jesus's intercession, Peter's faith did not fail. Likewise, our sins and failings make us vulnerable to Satan's accusations, but we have the prayers of Christ on our behalf. *"Christ…is even at the right hand of God, who also makes intercession for us"* (Romans 8:34). *"We have a great high priest…, Jesus the Son of God…. [He can] be touched with the feeling of our infirmities, [and] was in all points tempted like as we are, yet without sin"* (Hebrews 4:14–15). *"He ever lives to make intercession for [us]"* (Hebrews 7:25). Jesus is the only One in history who could say, *"The prince of this world comes, and has nothing in Me"* (John 14:30). Jesus's motives are always beyond question, His actions are always above reproach, and He is praying and working on our behalf.

I believe that, years after this interchange with Jesus, when Peter was writing to a group of Christians who were being persecuted, he remembered the attack of Satan. Wanting to encourage them to hold on to their faith, he called the devil an enemy who prowls around like a lion, looking for someone to devour, and he warned the believers to be alert to him. (See 1 Peter 5:8.) Peter knew by personal experience what it meant to be shaken in the grip of Satan.

Self-confidence is a noble trait only if we realize that our strength is in Christ. We must stand before God on the basis of the righteousness of Christ, not our own righteousness. *"For we... worship God in the Spirit, and rejoice in Christ Jesus, and have no confidence in the flesh"* (Philippians 3:3).

Satan hasn't been granted the power to devour the children of God, but he can influence us to the point of making us serve his ends if we don't watch and pray. He is a ruthless, merciless fiend whose goal is to defeat and destroy us. He should never be taken lightly.

If you yield to Satan, his evil influence can affect your health, moods, thoughts, and imagination. Why did Judas Iscariot betray Jesus and finally commit suicide instead of repenting? He allowed himself to listen to the temptations and lies of the enemy. The Bible tells us, *"Then entered Satan into Judas..., being of the number of the twelve. And he went his way, and communed with the chief priests and captains, how he might betray Him to them"* (Luke 22:3–4). After his betrayal, when the impact of what he had done hit him, Judas took his own life instead of repenting. Judas's response is in clear contrast with Peter's, who repented and was restored.

We cannot make the mistake of minimizing Satan's power or denying the reality of his kingdom of evil. But we must also avoid the error of falling into the devil's condemnation and losing our faith and trust in our heavenly Father. Remember that the enemy cannot go beyond the limits set by God. If we do fall into his deceitful traps and sin, we can repent and receive forgiveness through the blood of Christ. The born-again believer who submits to God and resists the devil will cause him to flee. (See James 4:7.)

DAY 38

SOME FACTS ABOUT PENTECOST

E. W. KENYON

*The natural man receives not the things of the Spirit of God:
for they are foolishness to him: neither can he know them,
because they are spiritually discerned.*
—1 Corinthians. 2:14

Let me make this statement first and then we will prove it: No one who walked with Jesus during His three and one-half years of public ministry was born again, was a new creation, or had eternal life. No one under the first covenant had eternal life until the Day of Pentecost.

But someone asks, "Didn't the disciples believe in Jesus?" Yes, but not as their Substitute, not as their Savior who was going to die and rise again from the dead. They believed in Him as the Son of God, as a great Prophet, as the One who was going to redeem them from the Roman yoke and establish again a Jewish nation. They knew nothing of His substitutionary work.

In John 11:25–27, we read the story of Martha and Jesus's conversation about the dead Lazarus. Jesus said, *"I am the resurrection, and the life: he that believes in Me, though he were dead, yet shall he live: whosoever lives and believes in Me shall never die. Believe you this? She says to him, Yea, Lord: I believe that You are the Christ, the Son of God, which should come into the world."*

She did not believe in Him as a Savior. She did not believe in His redemption. They knew nothing of His redemptive work. He could not make it clear to them.

The people who walked with Jesus did not know that He was going to rise from the dead, and even after He arose they did not believe it. They knew nothing about righteousness, of the ability to stand in the Father's presence without condemnation. They knew nothing of fellowship with the Father and with Jesus Christ. They had never had fellowship with the Master, any more than an unsaved man today can have fellowship with a child of God. They knew nothing of Sonship or of the family of God.

They were Jews under Law; servants, nothing more. They knew nothing of the Father in reality. He was just God to them. They knew nothing of the indwelling presence of the Holy Spirit. They didn't understand what John the Baptist meant when he said, *"He that comes after me is mightier than I, whose shoes I am not worthy to bear: He shall baptize you with the Holy Ghost, and with fire"* (Matthew 3:11).

Now read Acts 2:1–4:

When the day of Pentecost was fully come, they were all with one accord in one place. And suddenly there came a sound from heaven as of a rushing mighty wind, and it filled all the house where they were sitting. And there appeared to them cloven tongues like as of fire, and it sat upon each of them. And they were all filled with the Holy Ghost, and began to speak with other tongues, as the Spirit gave them utterance.

The Holy Spirit filled that upper room where they were sitting, and they were all immersed in the Holy Spirit. In other words, they were all recreated, received eternal life.

The second thing that happened: *"There appeared to them cloven tongues like as of fire, and it sat upon each of them."* Those tongues of fire showed that the gospel was going to be preached by men with tongues of fire, a message that could not be withstood. Stephen was the first man who paid the penalty of having a tongue of fire. They stoned him to death.

The third thing that happened in that upper room: *"They were all filled with the Holy Ghost."* You understand they could not receive the Holy Spirit until they were recreated. Before his death, Jesus had said, *"For He dwells with you, and shall be in you"* (John 14:17). They did not understand Him, but now the reality of the thing has come. They have been recreated. They have received the nature and the life of God. Now the Spirit is going to take them over. He is going to use their vocal chords to speak His own message.

Then the fourth amazing thing took place: *"They…began to speak with other tongues, as the Spirit gave them utterance."*

It is very important that we realize this: the disciples are entering into things of which they had no conception whatever. You can understand now what is meant when Jesus said that they were to be baptized in the Spirit. That immersion had meant their receiving eternal life, their union with Deity. It meant that the body of Christ had been brought into being. The thing we call the *ecclesia*, the church, had now become a real thing in the world. God's sons and daughters were in that upper room where only servants had been a few hours before.

DAY 39

PENTECOST GAVE US KEYS

REINHARD BONNKE

And I will give to you the keys of the kingdom of heaven: and
whatsoever you shall bind on earth shall be bound in heaven:
and whatsoever you shall loose on earth shall be loosed in heaven.
—Matthew 16:19

The Christian age is the power age. In the Old Testament, we read of the God of wonders performing marvels at the Red Sea, and under Elijah and Elisha. But not much more stands out in the thirty-nine books of the Old Testament except that on occasion, the power of the Holy Spirit fell upon a few individuals and the prophets. Then Jesus gave Peter the keys of the kingdom of heaven! Those keys are not jangling from Peter's belt at his post beside the pearly gates—the keys are the gospel of Christ crucified and the Holy Spirit. He opened the kingdom—and today we have the same keys. Peter saw what nobody on earth had ever seen before: three thousand people in one day turning in repentance and being born again by the Holy Spirit. Then the apostles went out and put the power of those keys to the test. The dead were raised; the deaf, blind, and crippled restored to full health; multitudes turned to Christ, and a new thing arose in the world: the church of Jesus Christ.

Pentecost is the giving of the Holy Spirit to the world in manifest form. It is God at work in the physical and material world. We only know of one form of the Spirit, and that is in manifestation. There is no "resting" Spirit, no Spirit in quiescence. The essence of Pentecost is the moving of the Spirit—the mighty wind from heaven and the flaming tongues of fire. The Holy Spirit is only known at work. There is no Spirit without movement, any more than there is a wind without movement. A wind that does not blow is not a wind at all. Wind is never quiet, or just an atmosphere. The Holy Spirit is a gale, and nobody can stand still in a force-eight gale and talk politely about the atmosphere! Where the Spirit is there is action, the miraculous—God in operation!

Any talk of miracles as "belonging to the past" denies the very purpose and nature of the gospel, as well as the character of the Holy Spirit. The Spirit is sent to work in this world. Deny the miraculous, the power of the Holy Spirit, and you deny what Christianity is supposed to be: God's power in action in the present age of living men and women. That is what makes this age the Christian age. Perhaps we ought to call this *the Holy Spirit Age*! Let us live in this age to the full!

DAY 40

THE MIRACLE WORKER

F. F. BOSWORTH

I tell you the truth; it is expedient for you that I go away:
for if I go not away, the Comforter will not come to you;
but if I depart, I will send Him to you.
—John 16:7

In Christ, "*the true vine*" (John 15:1), there is all the life for our souls and bodies that we need; but how are we to possess and enjoy this life except by our union with the Vine? It is not apart from Him, but in Him, that "*you are complete*" (Colossians 2:10).

Substitution without union is not sufficient for our possession and enjoyment of the life of the Vine. If you need a miracle, get in tune with the Miracle Worker. We enjoy the life of the Vine by our perfect union with the Vine. Asking for healing while refusing to be led by the Spirit is like asking a carpenter to repair the house while refusing to let him in the house.

"*As many as touched* [Him] *were made perfectly whole*" (Matthew 14:36). You cannot touch Him with reservation; therefore, like the woman who pressed through the throng and touched Him (see Luke 8:43–48), you must "elbow" out of your way, and press beyond selfishness, disobedience, unconfessed sins, lukewarmness, public opinion, traditions of men, articles written against divine healing—in fact, you must often press beyond your own pastor, who may be unenlightened in this part of the gospel—press beyond doubts, double-mindedness, symptoms, feelings, and the lying serpent.

The Holy Spirit, who is sent to execute for us the blessings of redemption, is our Paraclete, or Helper, and is ready to help us to press through and beyond all of these obstacles to the place where we can touch Him for our needs. God is waiting to pour out the Holy Spirit in fullness upon us. He comes as Christ's Executive to execute for us all the blessings provided by Calvary.

It is still true that as many as touch Him are made whole. How do we touch Him? By believing His promise. This is an infallible way of touching Christ for anything He has promised. We touch Him by asking, and by believing that He hears our prayers when we pray. When the woman touched Him, it was her faith that made her whole, not a mere physical touch (Luke 8:48); for *"the flesh profits nothing"* (John 6:63), *"but the Spirit gives life"* (2 Corinthians 3:6). Millions of sinners have thus touched Him for the yet greater miracle of the new birth.

As the sick touched Christ and were made whole when He walked upon the earth, so, now, it is the privilege of all actually to touch Him, and the touch now unites us to Christ in a closer union than it did then. This is not mere contact, but union as real as a branch and a vine. All that is in the Vine, including both spiritual and physical life, belongs to us—the branches.

The touch by faith can now bring us under the full control of the Holy Spirit, who is the Miracle Worker, as it could not do during Christ's earthly ministry, for the Spirit *"was not yet given"* (John 7:39). Jesus is not less a Savior and Healer since being glorified; He is *greater*. The privilege of touching Him now is much greater than when He was here in person, because more can now be received by the touch. From God's right hand, He has more to give; therefore, He said, "*It is expedient* [profitable] *for you that I go away*" (John 16:7). Since the Spirit comes to reveal Christ as He could not be revealed before He went away to send the Spirit, why can we not approach Christ for healing now with at least as much faith as those who thronged Him in that day?

The preceding shows the great importance of being right with God before asking for healing. The blessing of being right with God is a thousand times more desirable and enjoyable than the healing itself.

DAY 41

ANOINTED WITH POWER TO HEAL

MARILYN HICKEY

The Spirit of the Lord GOD is upon me; because the LORD has anointed me to preach good tidings to the meek; he has sent me to bind up the brokenhearted, to proclaim liberty to the captives, and the opening of the prison to them that are bound.
—Isaiah 61:1

The Word tells us God anointed Jesus of Nazareth with the Holy Spirit and with power. After that anointing, Jesus *"went about doing good, and healing all that were oppressed of the devil; for God was with Him"* (Acts 10:38). I looked up the word in the Greek that is translated *"oppressed"* in this verse and found that it means "to dominate or exercise lordship." When Jesus healed people, He exercised His authority over Satan's domination and "lorded it over" sickness.

When you are sick, you are being oppressed, or dominated, by illness, because in Acts 10:38, the Word says those whom Jesus healed were oppressed by the devil. If sickness was the oppression, or domination, of the devil when Jesus was here on earth, it is still the oppression of the devil. Remember, it was Satan who set sickness in motion in the first place. It was he who poisoned the mainstream of human life at the beginning. Sickness, infirmity, and disease of any kind are the oppression of the devil. They are *always* his work:

> *Forasmuch then as the children are partakers of flesh and blood, He also Himself* [Jesus] *likewise took part of the same; that through death He might destroy him that had the power of death, that is, the devil; and deliver them who through fear of death were all their lifetime subject to bondage.*
>
> (Hebrews 2:14–15)

Jesus came to set at liberty those who were bruised because of Satan's bondage. Jesus Himself, after reading from the scroll of Isaiah, declared to the people in the synagogue at Nazareth that He was the One *"anointed"* to do this work (see Luke 4:18), and He proved it by healing all manner of sickness (see Luke 4:40–41). If you are suffering in some area of your body, Satan is exercising lordship over you; if you have cancer, it is dominating you; if you have AIDS, that thing has you bound. But praise the Lord that the anointing breaks the yoke! (See Isaiah 10:27.) Jesus has the power to free anyone who is under the lordship of Satan because Jesus is Lord:

> *The Spirit of the Lord GOD is upon me; because the LORD has anointed me to preach good tidings to the meek; he has sent me to bind up the brokenhearted, to proclaim liberty to the captives, and the opening of the prison to them that are bound.*　　　　　　　　　　　(Isaiah 61:1)

I have good news for you! Jesus has done all that the Word said He would do. Jesus, the anointed of God (the Christ), opened the prison doors and released those who had been taken captive in their bodies through sickness of any sort. The doors are still open; healing is available for you more than two thousand years later. Read 1 John 3:8, and you will find: "He that *commits sin is of the devil; for the devil sinned from the beginning. For this purpose the Son of God was manifested, that He might destroy the works of the devil.*" *Jesus* took lordship over sickness at Calvary when He loosened and broke the works of the devil. There's no doubt that sickness is still around, but its power has been broken, and Jesus is still healing bodies today.

DAY 42

EMPOWERED TO SERVE

SMITH WIGGLESWORTH

In those days, when the number of the disciples was multiplied,
there arose a murmuring of the Grecians against the Hebrews,
because their widows were neglected in the daily ministration.
Then the twelve called the multitude of the disciples to them, and
said, It is not reason that we should leave the word of God, and
serve tables. Wherefore, brethren, look you out among you seven
men of honest report, full of the Holy Ghost and wisdom, whom
we may appoint over this business.…. And the saying pleased the
whole multitude: and they chose Stephen, a man full of faith and
of the Holy Ghost, and Philip, and Prochorus, and Nicanor, and
Timon, and Parmenas, and Nicolas a proselyte of Antioch.
—Acts 6:1–3, 5

During the time of the early church, the disciples were hard
pressed in all areas. The things of the natural life could not be
attended to, and many were complaining about the neglect of their
widows. The disciples therefore decided on a plan, which was to
choose seven men to do the work—men who were *"full of the Holy*

Ghost." What a divine thought! No matter what kind of work was to be done, however menial it may have been, the person chosen had to be filled with the Holy Spirit. The plan of the church was that everything, even the things of the natural life, had to be sanctified unto God, for the church had to be a Holy Spirit church.

There is no stopping in the Spirit-filled life. We begin at the cross, the place of ignominy, shame, and death, and that very death brings the power of resurrection life. And, being filled with the Holy Spirit, we go on "*from glory to glory*" (2 Corinthians 3:18). Let us not forget that possessing the baptism in the Holy Spirit means that there must be an ever-increasing holiness in us. How the church needs divine anointing—God's presence and power so manifested that the world will know it! People know when the tide is flowing; they also know when it is ebbing.

The necessity that seven men be chosen for the position of serving tables was very evident. The disciples knew that these seven men were men ready for active service, and so they chose them. In Acts 6:5, we read, "*And the saying pleased the whole multitude: and they chose Stephen, a man full of faith and of the Holy Ghost, and Philip.*" There were five others listed, of course, but Stephen and Philip stand out most prominently in the Scriptures. Philip was a man so filled with the Holy Spirit that a revival always followed wherever he went. Stephen was a man so filled with divine power that, although serving tables might have been all right in the minds of the other disciples, God had a greater vision for him—a baptism of fire, of power, and of divine anointing—that took him on and on to the climax of his life, until he saw right into the open heavens.

Had we been there with the disciples at that time, I believe we would have heard them saying to each other, "Look here! Neither Stephen nor Philip are doing the work we called them to. If they do not attend to business, we will have to get someone else!" That was the natural way of thinking, but divine order is far above our finite planning. When we please God in our daily activities, we will always find in operation the fact that *"he who is faithful in that which is least* [God will make] *faithful also in much"* (Luke 16:10). We have such an example right here—a man chosen to serve tables who had such a revelation of the mind of Christ and of the depth and height of God that there was no pause in his experience, but a going forward with leaps and bounds.

God has privileged us in Christ Jesus to live above the ordinary human plane of life. Those who want to be ordinary and live on a lower plane can do so, but as for me, I will not! For the same anointing, the same zeal, the same Holy Spirit power that was at the command of Stephen and the apostles is at our command. We have the same God that Abraham had, that Elijah had, and we do not need to come short in any gift or grace. (See 1 Corinthians 1:7.) We may not possess the gifts as abiding gifts, but as we are full of the Holy Spirit and divine anointing, it is possible, when there is need, for God to manifest every gift of the Spirit through us. As I have already said, I do not mean by this that we should necessarily possess the gifts permanently, but there should be a manifestation of the gifts as God may choose to use us.

This ordinary man Stephen became mighty under the Holy Spirit's anointing, and now he stands supreme, in many ways, among the apostles. *"And Stephen, full of faith and power, did great wonders and miracles among the people"* (Acts 6:8). As we go deeper in God, He enlarges our understanding and places before us a wide-open door, and I am not surprised that this man chosen to serve tables was afterward called to a higher plane.

Oh, that we might be awakened to believe His Word, to understand the mind of the Spirit, for there is an inner place of whiteness and purity where we can see God. Stephen was just as ordinary a person as you and I, but he was in the place where God could so move upon him that he, in turn, could move everything before him. He began in a most humble place and ended in a blaze of glory. Beloved, dare to believe Christ!

DAY 43

HOW TO BE LED BY THE HOLY SPIRIT

GUILLERMO MALDONADO

*Likewise the Spirit also helps our infirmities: for we know not
what we should pray for as we ought: but the Spirit Itself makes
intercession for us with groanings which cannot be uttered.*
—Romans 8:26

God never intended for us to walk aimlessly, trying to please
Him without guidance or direction. Instead, He sent us the Holy
Spirit and equipped us with the ability to hear, feel, intuit, and
discern His atmosphere. You too can be guided by the Holy Spirit,
just as the early Christians were, by doing the following.

GIVE YOURSELF TO A LIFE OF CONSTANT PRAYER

The first key to being led by the Spirit of God is living a life
of constant prayer and communion with God, as Jesus did; this is
the formula for remaining in a supernatural state where our every
step is aligned with God's plans and will. Prayer is communication with the Father, through which we receive His guidance and

direction. And it is the Holy Spirit who enables us to express our deepest needs and requests to the Father.

YIELD AND SURRENDER TO THE SPIRIT

Yielding to the Spirit means obedience and surrender, trading the natural of man for the supernatural of God. It is an act that comes from our own will. The Holy Spirit does not make us do things by force, but He does instruct us. We must yield to God's instructions and surrender our unbelief, doubts, weaknesses, selfish desires, emotions, thoughts, and fears to the Holy Spirit.

Every time we die to our rights, Jesus Christ gives us His rights, the same ones He won on the cross of Calvary. This is the law of exchange in which the Lord tells us, "I am going to give you more power, but I want you to surrender your fears, doubts, and unbelief. I am going to give you more wisdom, but I want you to surrender your ambitions and personal agenda to Me." To yield and surrender to the Spirit is to let God be God, in us and through us.

The guidance of the Holy Spirit in our lives increases in accordance with the measure that we surrender to Him. *"He must increase, but I must decrease"* (John 3:30). The more we yield to God, the more the life of Christ will dwell in us. All of us have something to surrender to Him; it may be riches, wicked thoughts, discouragement, immaturity, inconsistency, unforgiveness, impure relationships, ambition, or other things. We cannot allow anything in our lives to become an idol or to get in the way of the Holy Spirit's work in us or through us.

WALK IN THE SPIRIT, AND NOT THE FLESH

During the course of our lives, we will always face conflicts between our spirit and our flesh because *"the spirit indeed is willing, but the flesh is weak"* (Matthew 26:41). As human beings, we have three dimensions—spirit, soul, and body. A child of God who is led and influenced by the Holy Spirit operates from the first dimension, which is that of the spirit. Our spiritual man is formed when we are born again and is developed by obedience to the Word and being led by the Holy Spirit; this is the perfect balance in the spiritual realm. The spiritual man wants more of God and less of himself; therefore, he longs for the guidance of the Holy Spirit.

Those who live in the flesh operate in the second dimension of their humanity—the soul, which is the place where perversions are born. That is why they are selfish, self-absorbed, ambitious, and undisciplined, having uncontrollable appetites. They want more of themselves and less of God.

If you are fighting with matters of the flesh, go to the cross. That is the place where Jesus died, where He paid the price for our redemption and released His power upon us to overcome the flesh. Crucifying the flesh is part of our priesthood, of presenting ourselves as a living sacrifice before God and leaving our old nature at the altar. (See Romans 12:1.) This new priesthood comes in the form of spiritual offerings like praying, fasting, giving, and worshipping. When we are in that state of sacrifice, the Holy Spirit can speak to our inner being, lead us to all truth and to the will of God, and release His power over us. We must sacrifice our old man, or old nature, in order for our new spiritual man to live.

Today, I challenge you to let yourself be guided by the Holy Spirit—to acknowledge His impressions and intuitions and to hear and obey His voice. God wants you to manifest His power on earth. He sent His Spirit to be your Guide, to make His will known and to reveal His plans. You just have to surrender and yield to Him. Empty yourself by giving up your selfish will, your self-centered ambitions, and your human reasoning, and let God live in you. If today you say, "Holy Spirit, I want You to help me with my prayers, my marriage, my business and finances, and everything else," then He will guide you, and His influence in you will become stronger. He will place a desire in your heart to seek Him, to renounce your flesh, and to yield to Him. This is how you will become spiritually empowered and have a clear sense of direction in your life.

DAY 44

GREAT RESURRECTION POWER

CHARLES SPURGEON

But if the Spirit of Him that raised up Jesus from the dead dwell in you, He that raised up Christ from the dead shall also quicken your mortal bodies by His Spirit that dwells in you.
—Romans 8:11

If you have ever studied this subject, you have perhaps been rather perplexed to find that sometimes the resurrection of Christ is ascribed to Himself. By His own power and Godhead, He could not be held by the bond of death, but since He willingly gave up His life, He had the power to take it again. In another portion of Scripture you find the power ascribed to God the Father, "[God] *raised Him up from the dead*" (Acts 13:34). God the Father exalted Him. There are many similar passages. However, again, it is said in Scripture that Jesus Christ was raised by the Holy Spirit.

Now, all these things are true. He was raised by the Father because the Father said for Him to be loosed. Justice was satisfied. God's law required no more satisfaction. God gave an official message which delivered Jesus from the grave. Christ was raised by His own majesty and power because He had a right to come out. He could no longer be held by the bonds of death. However, He was raised after three days by the Spirit and the energy that His mortal frame received. If you want proof of this, open your Bibles again and read the following:

> For Christ also has once suffered for sins, the just for the unjust, that He might bring us to God, being put to death in the flesh, but quickened by the Spirit.   (1 Peter 3:18)

The resurrection of Christ, then, was effected by the agency of the Spirit. This is a noble illustration of His omnipotence.

Could you have stepped as angels into the grave of Jesus and seen His sleeping body, you would have found it to be as cold as any other corpse. If you had lifted up the hand, it would fall by the side. If you had looked at the eye, it would have been glazed. And, there was a death-thrust which must have annihilated life. Even if you had looked at His hands, you would have seen that the blood did not distill from them. They were cold and motionless.

Could that body live? Could it start up? Yes, and it is an illustration of the might of the Spirit. For when the power of the Spirit came on Him, as it was when it fell upon the dry bones of the valley, He arose in the majesty of His divinity. Bright and shining, He astonished the watchmen so that they fled away. He rose no more to die but to live forever, King of Kings and Prince of the kings of the earth.

One more work of the Spirit that will especially manifest His power is the general resurrection. From Scripture, we have reason to believe that while it will be effected by the voice of God and of His Word (the Son), the resurrection of the dead will be brought about by the Spirit. The same power that raised Jesus Christ from the dead will also quicken your mortal bodies. The power of the resurrection is perhaps one of the finest proofs of the works of the Spirit.

My friends, if this earth could but have its mantle torn away for a little while, if the green sod could be cut from it, and we could look about six feet deep into its bowels, what a world it would seem. What would we see? Bones, carcasses, rottenness, worms, corruption. And you would say, "Can these dry bones live? Can they start up?" Yes, *In a moment, in the twinkling of an eye, at the last trump: for the trumpet shall sound, and the dead shall be raised incorruptible, and we shall be changed* (1 Corinthians 15:52).

He speaks, and they are alive. See them scattered; bone comes to bone. See them naked; flesh comes upon them. See them still lifeless, *Come from the four winds, O breath, and breathe upon these slain, that they may live* (Ezekiel 37:9). When the wind of the Holy Spirit comes, they live, and they stand upon their feet as an exceedingly great army.

DAY 45

FAR MORE

CAROL MCLEOD

For this reason I bow my knees before the Father, from whom every family in heaven and on earth derives its name, that He would grant you, according to the riches of His glory, to be strengthened with power through His Spirit in the inner man, so that Christ may dwell in your hearts through faith; and that you, being rooted and grounded in love, may be able to comprehend with all the saints what is the breadth and length and height and depth, and to know the love of Christ which surpasses knowledge, that you may be filled up to all the fullness of God. Now to Him who is able to do far more abundantly beyond all that we ask or think, according to the power that works within us, to Him be the glory in the church and in Christ Jesus to all generations forever and ever. Amen.
—Ephesians 3:14–21 NASB

Paul, who had hunted down Christians and murdered them, had miraculously come to believe in Jesus as Messiah. He had been born into every advantage and benefit that the Jewish culture could offer—yet he laid it all aside for the sake of the call of Christ.

The apostle Paul ended up in a Roman prison cell because he had been found guilty of simply telling others about Jesus. While in prison, he wrote a letter to the church at Ephesus that is still changing lives today. This is Paul's compelling prayer:

Paul closed his extraordinary prayer above with such an exciting promise that it echoes through the hallways of Christendom even today: *"Now to Him who is able to do far more abundantly beyond all that we ask or think, according to the power that works within us"*!

Let's linger here for a minute to savor five of the most phenomenal words the Holy Spirit has ever written: *"far more abundantly beyond all."*

The richness of this Greek phrase, written by the hand of a man chained in a prison cell, presents a vivid and radical challenge to us.

Paul was unable to think of a word to describe what God was able to do in us and through us, so he made up his own word—one that is fifteen letters long! The word that Paul and the Holy Spirit collaborated on is *hyperekperissou*. This term can be translated as "superabundantly," "beyond measure," "exceedingly," or "far more than."[1]

Paul, the brilliant scholar and writer who was never at a loss for words, used this word three times, back-to-back, in rapid succession. And then, just for good measure, this academician and wordsmith added one smaller word for some extra punch. The word that he used as a grand exclamation point is *hyper*, which means "over," "beyond," or "more than."[2]

The absolute delight of this verse is that Paul is not exaggerating! All that you have ever prayed for and longed for is a possibility because of the One whose power is not limited by circumstances,

1. Rick Renner, *Sparkling Gems from the Greek*, vol. 1 (Tulsa: OK, self-published, 2003).
2. Ibid.

people, or time. All that you have ever asked for and dreamed about is probable because the God you serve is great enough to pull it off! God is capable of accomplishing far more than you could ever ask for or imagine. You can never out-dream God…but I dare you to try!

My friend, your biggest, most gargantuan dreams are smaller than God's tiniest plans for your life.

Paul's God is your God! The same power that was at Paul's disposal two thousand years ago is yours today! Remember that Paul wrote this riveting and enthusiastic prayer from a Roman prison cell. The chains that held Paul's feet in bondage had no ability to paralyze the power that was coursing through Paul's body.

God has called you to live a life so unrivaled that you will undoubtedly need His power to fulfill your earthly purposes. There is no such thing as an "impossible dream" because you serve a God to whom nothing is impossible. You honor God when you dream colossal dreams and when you pray "unrealistic" prayers. When you do so, He never thinks His child is being presumptive in prayer. The sad truth is that most of us are guilty of asking for far too *little*. Whatever we ask, think, or imagine—we serve a God who is able to do exceedingly and abundantly *more*.

Dunamis is the Greek word for *"power"* that Paul and the Holy Spirit used in the letter to the Ephesians.

It was *dunamis* power that raised Christ Jesus from the dead, and that same power is working within you.

It was *dunamis* power that was given to the disciples at Pentecost, and that same power is working within you.

Dunamis power is unable to lie dormant. *Dunamis* power is always working and is ever energetic. The *dunamis* power of God was given to show off His magnificence in your life even in your worst moments. Your life was always meant to be the grand demonstration of God's *dunamis* power!

DAY 46

STANDING IN THE GAP

MARY K. BAXTER

The people of the land have used oppression, and exercised robbery, and have vexed the poor and needy: yea, they have oppressed the stranger wrongfully. And I sought for a man among them, that should make up the hedge, and stand in the gap before Me for the land, that I should not destroy it: but I found none.
—Ezekiel 22:29–30

God has been bringing back to my remembrance many of the things that He showed me originally when I wrote the book *A Divine Revelation of Hell*. He has been revealing to me that we are in a time of the greatest move of God, but it is also a time when many people in our society have lost reverence for God. There are all kinds of perversions, widespread hatred, and frequent murders. Even many ministers are developing a mind-set of "anything goes."

Today, we are in great need of real intercessors—those who will *"stand in the gap"* and pray for our country and our world.

Prayer has the power to set the captives free because it connects the intercessor to the All-powerful One. When you encounter a person who is accustomed to speaking to God and hearing from Him, you find an individual ready to roll up his or her spiritual sleeves of prayer and fight the good fight of faith without hesitation.

Let us look at some of the attitudes and qualities that are essential in believers who want to be effective in intercession.

First, as intercessors, we must understand that Jesus and the Holy Spirit are interceding for us, and that when we intercede, we need to be aligned with God's will.

[Jesus], *because He continues ever, has an unchangeable priesthood. Wherefore He is able also to save them to the uttermost that come to God by Him, seeing He ever lives to make intercession for them. For such a high priest became us, who is holy, harmless, undefiled, separate from sinners, and made higher than the heavens.* (Hebrews 7:24–26)

The book of Hebrews tells us that Jesus, as our High Priest, is right now seated *"on the right hand of the throne of the Majesty in the heavens"* (Hebrews 8:1). He sacrificed Himself on our behalf, and now that He has returned to the Father, He is interceding for our spiritual preservation. In a revealing passage from John 17:9–24, where Jesus prayed to the Father just before His crucifixion, our Savior asked (1) that believers would live in unity, just as He is one with the Father, (2) that we would have the same joy He has, (3) that we would be kept from the evil one, (4) that we would be sanctified by God's truth, (5) that we would have unity with other believers and with the Father and the Son, (6) that we would be witnesses to the world of the truth of the gospel because of this unity, and (7) that one day we would live with Jesus and see His glory.

As we pray, we can intercede along the same lines for ourselves and others. Jesus said that we can pray to the Father in His name, and that our requests will be answered:

If two of you shall agree on earth as touching any thing that they shall ask, it shall be done for them of My Father which is in heaven. For where two or three are gathered together in My name, there am I in the midst of them. (Matthew 18:19–20)

He that believes on Me, the works that I do shall he do also; and greater works than these shall he do; because I go to My Father. And whatsoever you shall ask in My name, that will I do, that the Father may be glorified in the Son. If you shall ask any thing in My name, I will do it. (John 14:12–14)

You have not chosen Me, but I have chosen you, and ordained you, that you should go and bring forth fruit, and that your fruit should remain: that whatsoever you shall ask of the Father in My name, He may give it you. (John 15:16)

The Bible also assures us that God's Holy Spirit intercedes for us:

Likewise the Spirit also helps our infirmities: for we know not what we should pray for as we ought: but the Spirit Itself makes intercession for us with groanings which cannot be uttered. And He that searches the hearts knows what is the mind of the Spirit, because He makes intercession for the saints according to the will of God. (Romans 8:26–27)

When we are at a loss for words, the Holy Spirit steps in to intercede on our behalf. He communicates what we would pray if we only had the understanding and the words to say it. We should never view prayer as a laborious task because the Spirit is there to help us.

DAY 47

GOD'S PATTERN FOR A MODERN REVIVAL

AIMEE SEMPLE MCPHERSON

Then Philip went down to the city of Samaria, and preached Christ to them. And the people with one accord gave heed to those things which Philip spoke, hearing and seeing the miracles which he did. For unclean spirits, crying with loud voice, came out of many that were possessed with them: and many taken with palsies, and that were lame, were healed. And there was great joy in that city.
—Acts 8:5–8

The biblical pattern for a model revival is given us in the eighth chapter of the book of Acts. This revival reaches, as all model revivals should, in three directions, touching body, soul, and spirit. Its teachings ring forth clearly, declaring a triune God for a triune man. Its methods are simple, practical, powerful, and effective in bringing thousands to Christ.

Its threefold theme and presentation of Jesus Christ embraces salvation, divine healing, and the baptism of the Holy Spirit; a revival that fails to teach and see results along these three lines is more or less a failure and falls short of the biblical pattern of a model revival.

There were no great committee promotion boards or earthly organizations to assist Philip. There were no mammoth preparations made. In fact, a revival and a turning to Jesus Christ was farthest from the minds of the people of that city, and yet, the logical, Spirit-filled, Christ-exalting preaching of one man, accompanied by the demonstration and power of the Holy Spirit that backed up the Word, brought about such a soul-shaking revival that it turned the city upside down; caused the castles of doubt, superstition, and sin to fall crumbling to the dust; and swept thousands into the kingdom.

There is nothing mysterious, hidden, or beyond spiritual comprehension in the methods Philip used in bringing it about. He had the God-given pattern of the Word. He laid it on the whole cloth of that city and, with the scissors of the Holy Spirit, cut true to form.

We are told what steps led up to the revival, what brought the crowds of people together, what made them believe when they did come, and what happened when they did believe. We are given a complete pattern. Why should we not, therefore, pray to God for such a model revival of old-time power today as shook Samaria in the days of old?

"But what is the good of all this?" you ask. "What is the ultimate result of these healings of the body? Will they not ultimately go down into the grave, anyway? Would it not be better to do a work for the spirit, which lives forever?"

But do you not see, dear heart, that this is just what did happen? The healing of the body brought the people to Christ. *"When they believed Philip preaching the things concerning the kingdom of God, and the name of Jesus Christ, they were baptized, both men and women"* (Acts 8:12).

Divine healing served as the handmaiden of the gospel. Divine healing was the turnkey who went ahead to the doors of doubting castle and swung them upon their creaking hinges so that the Son of Righteousness might enter in with healing in His wings, drive back the dominion of night, and set the prisoners of darkness free.

The very Christ whose own ministry had been so marked with His healing of the sick and who asked, *"Which is easier, to say, Your sins be forgiven you; or to say, Arise, and walk?"* (Matthew 9:5), was with Philip, confirming the preached Word with signs following, and there was nothing left to do but believe.

These were not mere empty theories. These were practical, tangible facts and realities. A living Christ was being preached unto them, who had the power and the willingness to change their lives from darkness into light, to lift their burdens, to heal their sick, to banish their sin, and to clothe them with righteousness and joy.

Who could resist such a mighty Christ or withstand such a convincing argument? Not Samaria, at least—so the whole city turned to Christ.

Now we today, having our hearts cleansed by the precious, atoning blood of Jesus, having faith within us and such a baptism of Holy Spirit power as that which Philip received on the day of Pentecost, may still go forth, preaching the Word of God with boldness, and see our Christ confirm the Word with signs following, thus bringing multitudes to His feet. We should be able not only to preach about this power; we should also see it demonstrated in our midst, as Philip did in Acts 8:7, as Peter did in Acts 5:14–16, and as Paul did in Acts 28:8–9, when, by this means, they turned thousands to the Christ.

What a glorious revival it was—multitudes saved, healed, and baptized in water—and great joy in the city!

DAY 48

SEATED IN HEAVENLY PLACES

KYNAN BRIDGES

[God] has raised us up together, and made us sit together in heavenly places in Christ Jesus.
—Ephesians 2:6

The first time I went to a large wedding in Africa, I realized the importance of seating arrangements. In African culture, just like many other cultures, where you are seated at a wedding says a lot about who you are. Those who are part of the bridal party sit at the head table. The most esteemed guests sit at the very front. This is one of the easiest ways to identify who is who. Likewise, being a Master of seating arrangements, God has seated us together with Christ Jesus in the heavenly places. What does that mean, exactly? It means that we are part of the royal family. That's right! We are no longer outsiders. Through the blood of Jesus Christ, we have become *"heirs of God, and joint-heirs with Christ"* (Romans 8:17). This fact is absolutely amazing.

We are a part of the family of God, significant in Him. The problem is that "religion" has sold us a lie. We have been taught that we are nothing. We have been taught that we have no value. We have been taught that we are worthless. But that is not the case for the redeemed in Christ. Not only are we seated together with Him in heavenly places, but we are also exalted far above all principalities and powers. (See Ephesians 1:20–21.) No demon in hell is invited to this table. Why, then, do we entertain the lies of the enemy? He doesn't want us to know where we're seated. He wants us to believe that we are something other than what God says we are. But if we will simply grab hold of this truth by faith, our lives will never be the same.

God is calling you into a radical experience with His Spirit. This radical experience begins with an understanding of your true identity. When you realize you are a son or daughter of the Most High God, the spirit of vain tradition or religion will lose its power over you. It's time to change the way you think. It's time to think like a King's kid! Don't allow the enemy to keep you in bondage.

I'm a frequent traveler—not only within the United States, but also overseas. In fact, I probably spend more time in the air than I do on the ground. Okay, that's an exaggeration! But the point is that I've had my share of experiencing international travel. I will never forget the time I traveled to England and realized upon arrival that my bags had not arrived with me. All of my suits and ties, as well as other very important items, were in one of my suitcases. Even though I had arrived at my destination, the things I needed while I was in England were still in America.

My bags had essentially been "arrested" and detained. Among the definitions of *arrest* are "to seize (someone) by legal authority and take them into custody," and "to stop or check (progress or a process)." The process of transporting my luggage to England had definitely been checked. It would take three days before my bags reached the UK. Even after they arrived, I had to go through a very frustrating and time-consuming process to retrieve them.

Similarly, many people have experienced the arresting of their destinies. The enemy of our souls is constantly seeking opportunities to waylay the purposes and assignments God has for our lives. The good news is that, similar to my bags, our lives have already been "tagged" for our destinations. The airlines use tagging to determine where people's bags and other belongings should go. You, my friend, are marked for spiritual purpose:

> *In whom also we have obtained an inheritance, being predestinated according to the purpose of Him who works all things after the counsel of His own will.* (Ephesians 1:11)

You are a child of the King, and by the grace of God, you will arrive at your destination!

> Father, I thank You that I am a child of the King. I have been seated together with Jesus in heavenly places. In Christ, You have exalted me far above all principalities of darkness that would oppress or attack me. I declare that I am part of a "chosen generation" and a "royal priesthood." You called me out of darkness and into Your marvelous light. As a citizen of the kingdom of God, I exercise my rights of victorious living. I am more than a conqueror because You love me. I refuse to accept defeat as my portion. I declare that I am empowered to walk in my kingdom identity. I will never be a victim of fear, defeat, regret, depression, or despair. Power and grace are flowing in and through my life, to the glory of God. I declare that You are the lifter of my head. In Jesus's name, amen. (See 1 Peter 2:9; Romans 8:37; Psalm 3:3.)

DAY 49

THE SOURCE OF POWER FOR CHRISTIAN MISSIONS

HUDSON TAYLOR

My soul, wait you only upon God;
for my expectation is from Him.
—Psalm 62:5

The strength of a chain is limited to that of its weakest link. If, therefore, we are connected with the source of power by a chain, the weakest link will be the limit to which we can avail ourselves of it. But if our connection is direct and immediate, there is no hindrance to the exercise of the mighty power of God. *"My soul, wait you only upon God; for my expectation is from Him."*

God Himself is the great source of power. It is His possession. *"Power belongs to God"* (Psalm 62:11), and He manifests it according to His sovereign will. Yet, not in an erratic and arbitrary manner, but according to His declared purposes and promises. True, our opponents and hindrances are many and mighty, but our God, the living God, is Almighty. It is with Him that we have to do; on Him alone we have to wait; from Him alone cometh our salvation and our sufficiency.

Further, God tells us by His prophet Daniel, that *"the people that do know their God shall be strong, and do exploits. And they that understand among the people shall instruct many"* (Daniel 11:32–33). If it be ordinarily true that knowledge is power, it is supremely true in the case of the knowledge of God. Those who know their God do no *attempt* to do exploits, but *do* them. We shall search the Scriptures in vain, from Genesis to Revelation, for any command to *attempt* to do anything. God's commands are always "Do this." His prohibitions are always "Do not do this." If we believe the command to be from God, our only course is to obey, and the issue must always be success.

Further, God's power is available power. We are a supernatural people, born again by a supernatural birth, kept by a supernatural power, sustained on supernatural food, taught by a supernatural Teacher, from a supernatural book. We are led by a supernatural Captain in right paths to assured victories. The risen Savior, ere He ascended on high, said, *"All power is given to Me in heaven and in earth. Go you therefore…"*—disciple, baptize, teach all nations—*"…and, lo, I am with you always, even to the end of the world"* (Matthew 28:18–20).

Again, He said to His disciples, *"You shall receive power, after that the Holy Ghost is come upon you"* (Acts 1:8). Not many days after this, in answer to united and continued prayer, the Holy Ghost did come upon them and they were all filled. Praise God, He remains with us still. The power given is not a gift from the Holy Ghost. He, Himself, is the power. Today, He is as truly available, and as mighty in power, as He was on the day of Pentecost. But since the days before Pentecost, has the whole church ever put aside every other work, and waited upon Him for ten days, that that power might be manifest? Has there not been a cause of failure here? We have given too much attention to methods, and to machinery, and to resources, and too little to the source of power, the filling with the Holy Ghost. This, I think, has been the great weakness of our service in the past, and unless remedied will be the great weakness in the future. We are commanded to *"be filled with the Spirit"* (Ephesians 5:18). If we are not filled, we are living in disobedience and sin, and the cause of our sin, as the cause of Israel's sin of old, is the sin of unbelief. God is ready to fill us with the Holy Ghost, and to send us out all filled with the Holy Ghost to the uttermost ends of the earth. In answer to our prayers, mighty power may come upon our missionary laborers and native Christians in every quarter of the globe.

O, to have faith in the living God!

DAY 50

THE FULFILLMENT OF THE PROMISE

DEREK PRINCE

*For John truly baptized with water; but you shall be baptized
with the Holy Ghost not many days from now.*
—Acts 1:5

There is a direct parallel between the first creation and the new
creation. In the new creation, Jesus is the resurrected Lord and
Savior who conquered sin, death, hell, and Satan. Having done
this, He appeared to His disciples and breathed into them the
breath of resurrection life. This was a new kind of life, one that
had triumphed over all the forces of evil, death, and sin. Through
this experience of receiving the resurrection breath of life, the disciples passed out of the old order and entered into New Testament
salvation, into the new creation in Christ. However, it is important
to understand that even after this experience, the total fulfillment
of the promise of the Holy Spirit had not yet come.

After the resurrection, Jesus said to the disciples, *"Behold, I
send the promise of My Father upon you: but tarry you in the city*

of Jerusalem, until you be endued with power from on high" (Luke 24:49).

Even more explicitly, shortly before His ascension into heaven—and nearly forty days after Resurrection Sunday—Jesus said to them, *"For John truly baptized with water; but you shall be baptized with the Holy Ghost not many days from now"* (Acts 1:5). By this, we see that Resurrection Sunday was not the total fulfillment of the promise. Almost all theologians and commentators on Scripture agree that the final and complete fulfillment took place on the day of Pentecost, as described in Acts 2:1–4:

> *When the day of Pentecost was fully come, they were all with one accord in one place. And suddenly there came a sound from heaven as of a rushing mighty wind, and it filled all the house where they were sitting. And there appeared to them cloven tongues like as of fire, and it sat upon each of them. And they were all filled with the Holy Ghost, and began to speak with other tongues, as the Spirit gave them utterance.*

The events of Pentecost were the actual manifestation and fulfillment of the promise. The Holy Spirit descended from heaven, in person, in the form of a mighty wind. He filled each one of them individually, and gave each one a new and supernatural utterance in a language they had never learned. At the end of this second chapter of Acts, Peter gave a theological explanation of what had taken place:

> *This Jesus has God raised up, whereof we all are witnesses. Therefore being by the right hand of God exalted, and having received of the Father the promise of the Holy Ghost, He has shed forth this, which you now see and hear.* (Acts 2:32–33)

Please notice that all three persons of the Godhead are in this verse. Jesus the Son received the Holy Spirit from the Father and poured out the Holy Spirit on the disciples waiting in the upper room in Jerusalem. At that point, the final fulfillment of the promise of the coming of the Holy Spirit took place. The Holy Spirit Himself was released from heaven by the Father and descended upon the expectant disciples.

At this time, Jesus was not merely resurrected, but He was also exalted and glorified. In John 7:39, the writer of the gospel had pointed out that the promise of the Holy Spirit could not be fulfilled until Jesus had been glorified. We are therefore confronted with two dramatic, wonderful Sundays. The first is Resurrection Sunday, where we have the resurrected Christ and the inbreathed Spirit. The second is Pentecost Sunday, where we have the glorified Christ and the outpoured Spirit. Remember, each of these Sundays is a pattern for all believers—even today.

SOURCE MATERIAL

MARY K. BAXTER

The Enemy's Strategy (*A Divine Revelation of Spiritual Warfare*, coauthored by T. L. Lowery, Whitaker House, 2006, excerpted from chapter 3)

Standing in the Gap (*A Divine Revelation of Prayer*, coauthored by George Bloomer, Whitaker House, 2008, excerpted from chapter 8)

REINHARD BONNKE

God's "I Will" (*Faith, the Link to God's Power*, Whitaker House, 2014, excerpted from chapter 15)

Pentecost Gave Us the Keys (*Daily Fire Devotional*, Whitaker House, 2015, March 16 entry)

F. F. BOSWORTH

They Were Healed, Every One (*Christ the Healer*, Whitaker House, 2000, excerpted from chapter 3)

The Miracle Worker (*Christ the Healer*, Whitaker House, 2000, excerpted from chapter 5)

KYNAN BRIDGES

Supernatural Invasion (*Invading the Heavens*, Whitaker House, 2018, excerpted from chapter 14)

Seated in Heavenly Places (*90 Days of Breakthrough*, Whitaker House, 2018, excerpted from Days 16 and 69)

CHARLES FINNEY

The Holy Spirit's Role in Revival (*Experiencing Revival*, Whitaker House, 2000, excerpted from chapter 2)

JAMES W. GOLL

Holy Spirit, You Are Welcome Here! (*Passionate Pursuit*, Whitaker House, 2015, excerpted from chapter 7)

How the Holy Spirit Moves (*Releasing Spiritual Gifts Today*, Whitaker House, 2016, excerpted from chapter 2)

MARILYN HICKEY

The Anointing Breaks the Yoke (*Total Healing*, Whitaker House, 2011, excerpted from chapter 4)

Anointed with Power to Heal (*Total Healing*, Whitaker House, 2011, excerpted from chapter 5)

FRANCES HUNTER

Power to Heal (*God's Healing Promises*, Whitaker House, 2000, excerpted from pages 87–90)

JOAN HUNTER

Available to All Believers (*Miracle Maintenance*, Whitaker House, 2011, excerpted from chapter 10)

BILL JOHNSON

The Baptism of the Spirit Is for Power (previously unpublished material)

E. W. KENYON

God's Superman (*In His Presence*, Kenyon's Gospel Publishing, 1989, excerpted from chapter 5)

Some Facts about Pentecost (*New Creation Realities*, Kenyon's Gospel Publishing, 1989, excerpted from chapter 26)

JOHN G. LAKE

Does God Always Heal? (*John G. Lake on Healing*, Whitaker House, 2009, excerpted from chapter 17)

The Consciousness of Christianity (*The Flow of the Spirit*, Whitaker House, 2018, excerpted from chapter 11)

GUILLERMO MALDONADO

The River, the Waves, and the Flow of the Spirit (*Divine Encounter with the Holy Spirit*, Whitaker House, 2017, excerpted from chapter 8)

How to Receive an Outpouring of the Holy Spirit (*Baptism in the Holy Spirit*, ERJ Publishing, 2018, excerpted from chapter 3)

How to Be Led by the Holy Spirit (*Divine Encounter with the Holy Spirit*, Whitaker House, 2017, excerpted from chapter 7)

CAROL MCLEOD

Help Is On Its Way (*Stormproof*, Whitaker House, 2018, excerpted from chapter 7)

Far More (previously unpublished material)

AIMEE SEMPLE MCPHERSON

The Coming of the Holy Spirit (*This Is That*, Bridal Call Publishing House, 1919, excerpted from chapter 2)

God's Pattern for Modern Revival (*Divine Healing Sermons*, Whitaker House, 2014, excerpted from chapter 8)

JOSHUA MILLS

Keys to Receiving the Baptism of the Holy Spirit (*School of the Supernatural*, New Wine International, 2010)

The Anointing of the Holy Spirit (*Moving in Glory Realms*, Whitaker House, 2018, excerpted from chapter 2)

Working Miracles in the Spirit's Anointing (*Moving in Glory Realms*, Whitaker House, 2018, excerpted from chapter 6)

D. L. MOODY

Our Hearts, His Dwelling Place (*Secret Power*, Whitaker House, 2011, excerpted from chapters 1 and 4)

MYLES MUNROE

Ten Reasons to Speak in Tongues (*The Purpose and Power of the Holy Spirit*, Whitaker House, 2018, excerpted from chapter 12)

The Holy Spirit Poured Out at Pentecost (*The Purpose and Power of the Holy Spirit*, Whitaker House, 2018, excerpted from chapter 7)

ANDREW MURRAY

A Divine Outpouring (*The Spirit of Christ*, Whitaker House, 2018, excerpted from chapter 6)

The Twofold Blessing (*The Spirit of Christ*, Whitaker House, 2018, excerpted from chapter 1)

The Holy Spirit—The Spirit of Healing (*Divine Healing*, Whitaker House, 2019, excerpted from chapter 14)

DEREK PRINCE

The Significance of Pentecost (previously unpublished material)

Receiving the Inbreathed Spirit (*You Shall Receive Power*, Whitaker House, 2007, excerpted from chapter 5)

The Fulfillment of the Promise (*The Holy Spirit in You*, Whitaker House, 2019, excerpted from chapter 5)

WILLIAM SEYMOUR

Receive Ye the Holy Ghost (from 1907 sermon)

CHARLES SPURGEON

Great Resurrection Power (*Holy Spirit Power*, Whitaker House, 2001, excerpted from chapter 2)

LESTER SUMRALL

The Gift of Tongues (*The Gifts and Ministries of the Holy Spirit*, Whitaker House, 2005, excerpted from chapter 9)

The Charismatic Renewal (*The Gifts and Ministries of the Holy Spirit*, Whitaker House, 2005, excerpted from chapter 2)

HUDSON TAYLOR

The Source of Power for Christian Missions (from an address delivered at the Ecumenical Conference in Carnegie Hall, New York, Monday, April 23, 1900)

R. A. TORREY

The Person of the Holy Spirit (*The Presence and Work of the Holy Spirit*, Whitaker House, 2004, excerpted from chapter 1)

JOHN WESLEY
On the Holy Spirit (*Sermons on Several Occasions*, 1771, excerpted from sermon 141)

SMITH WIGGLESWORTH
The Fullness of the Spirit (*Smith Wigglesworth on the Holy Spirit*, Whitaker House, 1999, excerpted from chapter 3)

Brokenness Precedes Blessing (*Smith Wigglesworth on Spirit-Filled Living*, Whitaker House, 1998, excerpted from chapter 18)

Empowered to Serve (*Smith Wigglesworth Only Believe*, Whitaker House, 2006, excerpted from chapter 2)

MARIA WOODWORTH-ETTER
The Spirit Reveals the Deep Things of God (*The Holy Spirit*, Whitaker House, 1998, excerpted from chapter 1)

The Spirit Comes in Many Ways (*The Holy Spirit*, Whitaker House, 1998, excerpted from chapter 3)